GREAT IRISH SPORTS STARS

CORA
STAUNTON

D1637874

Photograph by Selina O'Meara

EIMEAR RYAN is from County Tipperary and lives in Cork. She writes about sport for the *Irish Examiner* and is an editor for the literary journal *Banshee*. Her writing has appeared in *Winter Papers*, *Granta*, *The Dublin Review*, *The Stinging Fly*, *Town & Country* (Faber) and *The Long Gaze Back* (New Island). Eimear plays camogie for St Finbarr's in Cork. She was never much good at ladies football but she loves watching the game. This is her first book for young readers.

GREAT IRISH SPORTS STARS

CORA STAUNTON

EIMEAR RYAN

THE O'BRIEN PRESS
DUBLIN

For Doireann, Aoife & Éanna

First published 2019 by
The O'Brien Press Ltd,
12 Terenure Road East, Rathgar,
Dublin 6, D06 HD27 Ireland.
Tel: +353 1 4923333; Fax: +353 1 4922777
E-mail: books@obrien.ie.
Website: www.obrien.ie.
The O'Brien Press is a member of Publishing Ireland

ISBN: 978-1-78849-105-1

9 8 7 6 5 4 3 2 1
23 22 21 20 19

Printed in the UK by Clays Ltd, Elcograf S.p.A.
The paper in this book is produced using pulp from managed forests.

Published in:
DUBLIN
UNESCO
City of Literature

CONTENTS

CARNACON

I t was three weeks before Christmas and Cora Staunton still hadn't a single present bought. All her focus had been on the game in Parnell Park. Her club, Carnacon, was playing Mourneabbey in the All-Ireland club football final. It was a cold day for football, but Cora didn't mind. She happily played in any weather: wind, rain or shine.

Cora was wearing green and red, as usual. Carnacon had the same colours as her county: Mayo. At this stage, the green and red jersey was like a second skin.

Even though she'd played in several All-Ireland finals, both club and intercounty, she still got nervous before the game. She bounced on the balls of her feet in the tunnel before the teams ran out on the pitch, her studs clattering off the concrete.

'The butterflies never really go away, sure they don't?' she said to her friend, Fiona McHale. Cora and Fiona had played together for years, both with Carnacon and Mayo. They always had each other's backs.

'You need the butterflies,' said Fiona. 'They mean you're ready to play.'

Cora nodded in agreement as they ran out onto the pitch. She knew that people expected a lot from her. Her teammates, management, the supporters – they all looked to her to score. The way she saw it, scoring was her job. It had always been her job, ever since she was a kid. Every back who marked her wanted to stop her from doing what she did best. Over the years, she'd worked hard on her skills to make herself as difficult to mark as possible. She could score off her right foot, her left foot, her fist, from placed ball or from play. She knew she would need to draw on all her abilities to win today.

The game got off to a frantic start. Mourne-abbey had lost a couple of finals in the last few years and were determined to come out winners.

But Carnacon were equally hungry. Cora missed the first free kick she got, but she didn't panic. She knew that confidence was everything. *Next ball,* she told herself. And sure enough, the next ball she got she kicked over the bar.

She got another score before half-time. Going into the break, Carnacon were leading, but only just. In the dressing room, everyone was tense.

'We're up by three points, girls,' said Fiona. 'Let's just keep it going, okay? Let's keep working hard.'

They'd played some good football in the first half, but they had also kicked a lot of wides. The nerves of playing a big match were getting to them.

The last All-Ireland that Cora played was a difficult one. It was the previous September, in Croke Park. When Cora was a kid she used to dream of playing on that pitch. She'd played there several times by now, but it still sent a tingle up her spine every time she ran out onto the grass. That day in September, Mayo lost to Dublin in the All-Ireland final. Cora had tried her hardest and scored seven points, but Dublin were on fire. There was no stopping them. All Cora knew now was that she didn't want to be on the losing side again. Not today.

The panel got in a huddle and the players put their arms around each other. Cora studied the faces of the other girls. Some of these players she'd known for years: Fiona, Michelle, Martha, Sharon. Some were teenagers, around the same age she was when she started playing senior football: Amy, Louise, Sadhbh. Cora looked them all in the eye. In everyone's expression, she saw the same trust and determination.

'Ask yourselves this, girls,' she said. 'In half an hour, when this is over, do ye want to be in here crying? Or do ye want to be in here with the cup?'

'With the cup!' they all shouted in unison.

Cora nodded, pleased. They were ready. She led them back down the tunnel.

Back out on the pitch, she swung her arms to warm up in the freezing weather. It was hard to believe that in a couple of days she'd be on a plane to sunny Sydney, Australia. She was going there to play Australian Rules Football for a team called the Greater Western Giants. This would be a new start for Cora, at age thirty-six. A new challenge. Even a new type of ball! She'd always aspired to playing sport full-time, dreamed of making a living from it, and now she had a chance to do just that. As a bonus, her brother Brian already lived in Sydney with his wife and two sons. Cora couldn't wait to see them all.

But she couldn't think about that just yet. She had a job to do.

Carnacon started the second half steadily and racked up a few scores to put themselves seven points in front. Mourneabbey came back strongly, however. The Cork team weren't going to be beaten easily. With ten minutes to go, Mourneabbey were on the attack. Cora watched with her heart in her mouth as they scored a brilliant goal. Carnacon's lead was now just three points.

'Heads up, girls,' she called to her teammates. 'Next ball!'

The ball bounced up the field and the Carnacon forwards worked hard to win a free. Looking around for an option, Cora spotted a loose teammate and kicked a short ball to her for a one-two. Cora received the ball back, rounded a Mourneabbey defender and fisted it over the bar. The Carnacon supporters roared, delighted with this response to the Mourneabbey goal.

Cora pressed on, scoring four of Carnacon's last five points. Mourneabbey fought back again, but she knew that if they just kept working hard –

Wham! She was hit by a late challenge. Cora went down, winded, her ribs sore. Her marker got a yellow card. Cora's teammates came over to her, concerned, not wanting to lose their captain at this important moment.

'I'm grand,' she reassured them. She just needed a few seconds to get her breath back. *You're nearly there*, she told herself. *Keep going.* She picked herself up and placed the ball for the free kick. She landed the ball over the bar to the cheers of the supporters.

The last few minutes of the game were frantic, with both sides desperately trying to get the upper hand. Three players were sent to the sin bin. Cora knew that it was now even more important to work hard and help out her teammates.

'We're nearly there, girls!' she shouted in encouragement. 'Nearly there!'

When the final whistle blew, Cora fell to her knees and pointed to the sky. Her teammate Doireann ran over and they hugged and danced around together.

There was no sweeter feeling than winning an All-Ireland final.

As captain, it was Cora's job to accept the trophy. She kissed the cup before lifting it. It was her sixth All-Ireland title with Carnacon. As a young football-mad girl growing up, she never imagined this level of success.

In just a few days, she'd fly out to Sydney. She was excited for her Australian adventure, but right now it was all about this moment. Her club, her friends, football. She couldn't wait to bring the cup back to Carnacon, where it all began.

CHAPTER 1

CORA'S FIRST MATCH

'See you at the match after school, Cora?'

Cora grinned back at the dark-haired boy calling to her across the playground. 'Definitely, Alan. See you then!'

Back in the classroom, Cora could barely sit still through the last few hours of the school day. Tonight, she'd be playing her first real football match with the local Under-12 team, Ballintubber. It was mostly boys on the team, but Cora didn't mind. She liked playing with them. They were funny and rough and some of them were really good footballers, like Alan Dillon, who played at centre-forward. Cora hoped to be playing alongside him later.

It was on the Carnacon National School pitch that she'd honed her football skills, encouraged by Mr Ó Súilleabháin, the principal. Football would have always been seen as a boys' sport, but Mr Ó Súilleabháin didn't think that way. It didn't matter to him if you were a boy or a girl – as long as you were up on the pitch playing sport.

Not everyone felt that way, though. Cora was friends with all the boys on the team now, but some of them had laughed when she first went to Under-12 training.

'This is a bit rough for girls,' one of them sneered. 'Why don't you go home and play with your dollies?'

Then they had seen her play. Cora was small, but she was fast. And she had skill. From the first time she picked up a football, she just knew what to do with it. She could kick the ball a fair distance, but she also knew that power wasn't everything. Sometimes you needed to kick a short pass or do a toe-to-hand, and that required a different sort of skill.

What Cora liked most about football, though, was how much she still had to learn. Every time she practised, she got a little bit better. She loved watching the Mayo footballers and her hero, Maurice Fitzgerald, on *The Sunday Game*. She was mad about Maurice – even though he was from Kerry, not Mayo. She watched him kick points from the sideline and thought, *Maybe one day I'll be able to do that.*

Cora got a lift to the game with her friend Michelle McGing, the only other girl on the team. When they arrived at the pitch, they went into the dressing room with the lads. One of their trainers hurriedly approached, an apologetic smile on her face.

'Sorry, girls. Ye'll have to tog out in the loo.'

Embarrassed, Cora and Michelle picked up their gear bags and retreated to the grimy toilet next to the dressing room. Cora didn't like being separated from the rest of the team.

'It's only because we're girls,' she said, as they put on their socks and boots.

'I know,' said Michelle.

They were both a bit annoyed, but when their trainer stuck her head around the door moments later and handed them their jerseys, they were delighted – number 5 for Michelle and number 13 for Cora.

'Unlucky thirteen,' Michelle said, teasing her.

Cora laughed. 'I'll have to make my own luck out there.'

Once they were togged out, the girls were allowed back into the dressing room for the team talk. Her first real game! Cora had butterflies fluttering in her stomach. She couldn't wait to run out on the pitch.

Ballintubber were the first team out on the field. Cora walked over to her position and swung her arms, getting ready for the game. She tucked some strands of her blonde bob behind her ears and reminded herself to bring a hairband next time, so it wouldn't get in her way. The opposition, Castlebar Mitchels, sprinted out onto the field in their red and yellow jerseys. Cora watched them closely. They were a big team – some of them were much taller than the Ballintubber players. She saw the cornerback come towards her. He towered over her.

When he was a few metres away, he stopped suddenly. 'Oh my god. I'm marking a *girl*.'

Cora laughed. 'Yeah. So what?'

The Castlebar boy ignored her. He shouted over to his goalkeeper. 'Can you believe this? A girl!' The two of them started laughing.

Now Cora was annoyed. 'What's your problem?'

'You are,' the corner-back replied. 'You shouldn't be here. Girls can't play football.'

'Yes, we can!'

'Oh yeah? Name one famous footballer who's a girl.'

Cora's heart sunk. It was true that there was no girl version of Maurice Fitzgerald. She knew female superstars in other sports – like Sonia O'Sullivan, her favourite runner – but she couldn't think of any women who were famous footballers. She wondered why this was. Maybe the corner-back was right. Maybe girls couldn't play football.

The ball was thrown up and the tall Castlebar boys won it over the heads of the Ballintubber players. They soloed down the pitch and scored a point. From the kickout they won it again, scored another. After fifteen minutes Castlebar were four points up and Cora hadn't even gotten a kick of the ball yet. She took a deep breath and reminded herself to be ready for the ball to break to her at any time.

Suddenly the play swung Ballintubber's way and they managed to work the ball up the field. Alan went deep into midfield and won it, then soloed through the forwardline. Cora broke away from her marker and ran alongside Alan, giving him an option. He handpassed it to her and she kicked it straight between the posts.

'Great stuff, Cora!' shouted Alan.

She gave him a thumbs-up and ran back to her place. As they were waiting for the ball to be kicked out, her marker gave her a shove.

'Hey!' she said.

'Even with that point, ye're still losing, you know,' he said, grinning.

Cora knew she shouldn't allow him to annoy her, but he did. She gritted her teeth. When half-time came she was grateful for the chance to cool off. She took a long drink of water.

'Don't mind him, Cora,' said Alan, who had noticed the corner-back's antics. 'You're miles better than him, you're way faster. You can turn him every time.'

She nodded. She knew that she needed to tune

out what her marker was saying to her. All that mattered was the ball.

Ballintubber started the second half well, winning a close-in free, which Alan put over the bar. Michelle attacked the kickout and charged forward with the ball. She kick-passed it to Alan, who added another point from play.

'Good stuff, Alan! Well done, Michelle!' Cora shouted.

The Castlebar keeper kicked it short and Alan won it this time. He soloed through the middle and Cora slipped inside her marker towards the square. Alan spotted her and handpassed it to her. Cora grabbed it, turned the full-back, and buried the ball in the back of the net.

What a feeling! She punched the air as she ran back outfield. Michelle came over for a high-five. When Cora picked up her marker again, all his smiles were gone.

Castlebar responded with a point to level it, but Ballintubber got another couple of points to secure their win. When the final whistle went, Cora turned to her marker and shook his hand.

'Well done, good game,' she said.

He didn't say anything. He couldn't even look her in the eye. Cora shrugged and went over to celebrate with her teammates.

★

Cora practically danced in the door with her gear bag.

'Mam? Dad?' she called.

She heard a commotion over her head as a few of her siblings ran down the stairs to meet her.

'How did you get on?' asked Collette, her big sister.

'We won!' Cora told her. 'I scored a goal!'

Her brothers cheered and Collette gave Cora a hug.

'That's brilliant, well done!' Collette was in secondary school already and played on the school basketball team. She knew how important sport was to Cora.

Cora went into the living room. Her dad was in an armchair by the fire, tired after a day's work on the farm.

'Did you hear we won, Dad?'

'I did, Cora.' He smiled. 'Sorry I couldn't be there.'

'That's okay.' She would have loved for her parents to be able to come see her play, but with eight kids in the family it was difficult. Besides, both of her parents worked long hours – her dad on the farm, her mam in the local hospital.

'Where's Mam?' she asked.

'In the kitchen,' her dad said. 'She kept some dinner for you.'

Cora dumped her gear bag in a corner and opened the door to the kitchen. Her mam was at the cooker with her back to Cora.

'Mam, did you hear we won?'

Cora's mam turned around, smiling. 'Of course I heard! Aren't you shouting it from the rafters?' She opened her arms for a hug. 'Well done, Cora. I'm so proud of you. Now, sit up at the table there for some dinner.'

Cora sat down, swinging her legs happily under the table. She described the goal she scored as she tucked into sausages and chips.

Her mam listened attentively, then suddenly looked concerned. 'Janey Mac, Cora. Is that a bruise I see?'

Cora looked down at her arm, where a big blue bruise was already forming. It must have been one of the times her marker shoved her.

'I'm grand,' she said. 'The lad I was marking was a bit rough, that's all.'

Cora's mam shook her head. 'Be careful, Cora, won't you? Those boys are way bigger than you. I worry about you sometimes. You're only a slip of a thing!'

Cora smiled. She hadn't even noticed the bruise until her mother saw it. 'Don't worry, Mam. I'm well able.'

CHAPTER 2

PRACTICE MAKES PERFECT

After playing her first proper game, Cora was hooked. Every spare minute she had at home – once homework and jobs for her mam were done – was spent out the back at the gable end of the house. It was a good wall to practise at because it only had one small window, high up – the bathroom window. Cora could spend hours there, kicking, kicking, kicking.

Her older brother Peter grinned at her as he came back from working on the farm. 'I'm surprised your right leg hasn't fallen off yet, Cora, with all the practice you're doing.'

She laughed, but his words stuck with her. Why was she doing all her practice on her right, anyway?

Sure, it was her natural foot, but Maurice Fitzgerald was able to kick off both feet – the commentators on telly were always talking about it. If she could learn to kick off her left foot as well, she'd have a huge advantage over her opponents.

The ball bounced back to her off the wall. It was a cheap plastic one she'd bought in a toy shop in Claremorris with her pocket money. She had a nice O'Neills leather ball that she'd gotten for her birthday – herself and her brother Brian sometimes had a kickaround with it – but she didn't want to ruin it by hopping it off the concrete wall. The plastic one had a good weight to it, and she didn't care if it got punctured, which made it perfect for practice.

She tried kicking the ball on her left foot. She connected okay, but the ball went straight up into the air instead of at the wall. It felt weird, too, like when she'd tried to write with her other hand in school one day – instead of neat, joined-up writing, she could only do a scrawl. She tried kicking off her left again. A bit better this time – the ball bounced off the wall – but it still felt strange and unfamiliar.

I'm going to practise off my left foot until it's as good

as my right, Cora promised herself. *Then there'll be no stopping me!*

She played in the yard for another twenty minutes until it started to get dark, soloing in loops around the trees, dodging imaginary opponents.

And Staunton wins it! She turns inside, she's flying towards the goals … In her head, she could hear the voice of Mícheál Ó Muircheartaigh, her favourite commentator. *Still Staunton, being chased! Forced onto her left side … she's going for goal!*

With that, Cora kicked it off her left on the run. This time she connected squarely with the ball. It was an incredibly satisfying feeling. She basked in it for a moment or two.

SMASH!

The small, high-up window shattered into a thousand pieces. From inside, Cora could hear a shriek. Someone must have been in the bathroom when she broke the window!

Peter heard the commotion and reappeared around the corner. 'Ah, Cora, what have you done?'

'It was my left foot!' she protested. 'I'm normally way more accurate!'

Peter picked up the football and threw it at her.

'You better run before whoever was in the bathroom catches you!'

Laughing, Cora caught the ball and ran down the yard to hide.

The next day at school, Cora was eager to practise kicking off her left in the safety of the wide, open playing pitch. However, Mr Ó Súillebháin announced that he wanted to see them practising basketball at lunchtime. There was an upcoming schools basketball tournament and he wanted them to be on top form.

Cora felt deflated. She had been waiting to play football all day! She enjoyed basketball, too – she enjoyed most sports she tried – but it didn't give her the same buzz as football.

She must have looked a bit reluctant out on the court, because Mr Ó Súilleabháin called her over.

'Are you all right, Cora? You're not your usual enthusiastic self!'

'Sorry, sir,' said Cora. 'It's just I was really looking forward to practising my football today and ...'

'Football, of course. Sorry, I forgot that you practise your football every Thursday. And every day
that ends in a "y".'

Cora looked at him. You could never be sure
whether Mr Ó Súilleabháin was being serious or
messing, because he was so good at keeping a straight
face. But she thought she saw a smile twitching at
the corner of his mouth.

'There aren't enough days in the week for football,' she said.

Mr Ó Súilleabháin burst out laughing. 'I admire
you, Cora. There aren't many ten-year-olds as
focused as you. But you know, there are other ways
to practise football besides kicking a ball around.'

'Like how?'

'Well, you can think about the game. Mental
preparation is really important, did you know that?'

Cora shook her head.

'If you can plan out in your head what you'll do
in a match in different situations – a high ball, a
low ball, a ball out at the sideline, straight in front
of goal – you'll find it way easier to do on the day.
You'll be a split second ahead of everyone else, too.
You'll have no hesitation, because you'll have *already*

decided what you're going to do.'

Cora nodded. This made sense to her, somehow.

'And believe it or not, you can practise football when you're playing other sports!'

Cora laughed. 'Ah, come off it, sir.'

'I'm serious! It's amazing what you can learn from other sports – both from watching and playing. Take soccer, now – you can learn a lot about movement from watching the Premiership. Have you seen those lads on the telly? They never stop running! Making runs here, making runs there. Nine times out of ten it's a dummy run, but the tenth time? That's when they get their goals.'

'Fair enough,' said Cora. She was always eager to learn how to score more goals.

Mr Ó Súilleabháin nodded towards the kids behind them, bouncing the ball up and down the court, calling to each other. 'And with basketball, you can learn about teamwork. See how the whole team works together as a unit? Instead of one person putting pressure on themselves to do all the scoring?' Cora wasn't sure, but she thought Mr Ó Súilleabháin gave her a little sideways grin. 'Basketball is all about giving the ball to the player in the best position. Play every sport you can, Cora, and then bring everything you learn to football.'

Cora stood a moment longer watching her class-mates. 'You really think this will make me a better footballer?'

'I know it, Cora.'

With that she ran back out on the court, won a loose ball and dribbled it towards the net. She might not get to practise her left foot today, but she could still improve.

CHAPTER 3

PLAYING WITH THE LADS

Cora laced her boots up in the stand of the Ballintubber pitch. Herself and Michelle were sitting next to each other on the concrete seats, while all around them, the lads joked and slagged and punched each other in the arm. There was a clatter as they all ran down the steps together in their studs, out onto the pitch.

Cora was really enjoying training with the lads. Her coach, Seán Hallinan, always put her on someone bigger and stronger during training matches; she figured it was his way of trying to make her better. So far, herself and Michelle were more than holding their own against the boys. At this stage, the boys just treated Cora as one of the lads – and if any of them ever said anything to her, she knew that her brothers Brian and David would stick up for her.

They started the session with two laps of the pitch followed by stretches to warm up. Then Seán upended a large bag of footballs. Cora always loved seeing them come spilling out onto the grass. They began a handpassing drill, passing the ball back and forth in pairs. Next, they did the same with kick-passing. Cora was careful to practise on both feet, even though it still felt pretty strange on her left.

Seán organised them into a high-catch drill. They lined up in pairs, and he threw the ball high in the air for each pair to compete for possession. Cora disliked high balls. She much preferred to gather the ball close to the ground, where she could control it and turn her marker in a flash.

Cora sighed. She was paired with Alan, who was way taller than her.

'Ah here,' she said, and Alan laughed.

'What's wrong, Cora?' Seán asked.

'Sure he's way bigger than me. Not much of a contest, is it?'

Seán shrugged. 'It could be like this in a game.

You have to learn to cope with it.' He had no pity for her.

'Don't worry, Cora,' said Alan. 'I'll let you catch one of them.'

'You will not,' she laughed, shoving him.

Seán threw up the ball between herself and Alan. Cora watched the flight of the ball, braced herself, and sprang. Her hands were so close … and then Alan plucked the ball easily out of the air from over her head.

'Ugh,' said Cora, pure frustration coming out of her.

Alan just smiled. 'It's grand to be tall.'

'I'd bate you off the pitch if I was the same size!'

Alan laughed. 'You talk a good game, anyway!'

Cora watched the other pairs competing for the ball, itching for her next chance.

'It's all about timing, Cora,' Seán said before throwing the ball up for them again.

This time, she tried to jump a split second before Alan. She felt her gloved fingers graze the ball, but again, Alan got that bit higher and got a grip of it.

'That was better, Cora,' Seán called in encouragement, but Cora was still frustrated.

Alan nudged her as they lined up again. 'Don't let it get to you so much. You're good at every other skill! Everyone has a weak spot.'

Cora just shook her head. 'I have to be the best.'

They reached the top of the line again, Seán in front of them with the ball.

'Remember now, Cora, it's all about timing.' He threw it up.

It was as if everything went into slow motion, like in the movies. This time, Cora didn't watch the ball; she watched Alan. She jumped as he jumped, but instead of reaching for the ball, she made sure to lean into his shoulder as he reached for the ball. It worked; he was knocked off balance, his hands grasping at air. Cora felt her feet touch the grass, and she let out a delighted laugh as the ball fell into her waiting hands.

'Good stuff, Cora!' said Seán. 'Now you're getting it.'

She handpassed the ball back to him, grinning. Turning to Alan, she saw the same frustrated look on his face that she must have been wearing a few minutes ago. He had the same competitive streak as her, she realised. Competing against him would make her a better player.

'Not bad for a shortie,' he said grudgingly as they took their place at the back of the group.

She laughed. 'So lookit, you've won two and I've won one, so the score's 2-1. Bet I can beat you to five ...'

'No way. You're going down, Staunton!'

She grinned. 'We'll see about that.'

Back in the stand, Cora put on her tracksuit top and her runners. Seán had promised her a lift home so she went back out onto the pitch to help him gather up the cones from the training session.

At the far end of the field she could see someone taking frees from the 20-metre line. The person had three footballs and was kicking them steadily over the black spot, like clockwork, before running behind the goals to gather the balls again. Cora couldn't make out who it was, but she could see that the freetaker had red hair tied back in a ponytail. It was a girl.

Cora jogged down to get a closer look, but she

felt suddenly shy. The girl was a proper grown-up, in her late twenties maybe.

'Do you want me to kick the ball back to you?' Cora asked.

The girl turned around and smiled at her. 'That'd be great, thanks.'

Cora recognised her then. 'Oh, hi Beatrice!'

Beatrice laughed, surprised. 'Cora, 'tis yourself!'

The freetaker was her old babysitter, but she hadn't minded Cora in years, now that Cora's older siblings were old enough to do the minding.

Cora ran behind the goals and started gathering the balls. When the ball dropped over the bar she tried to catch it before it bounced, practising her high catch.

They continued for five or ten minutes, the free-taker kicking, Cora catching. Eventually, Seán called Cora to say they'd be heading soon.

'Thanks for your help, Cora,' said Beatrice. 'I've been watching you play for the boys' team. You're a real flyer.'

'Thanks,' said Cora. She could feel herself blush-ing. She knew she was good, but it meant a lot when others told her. And Cora could see that

Beatrice was a decent player, too – she clearly knew her football.

'Do you play for Carnacon?' Cora asked. A local ladies football club had been started a few years previously, but they only had an adult team so far.

'I do indeed. I'm involved in coaching as well. You'll be playing alongside me before long, I'd say.'

Cora shrugged. 'I like playing with the lads.'

'I know. But you won't be able to do that forever, unfortunately.' Beatrice came closer. 'Have you thought about playing for the Carra under-13 girls team? They're entering in the Community Games, and I'm one of the mentors.'

'Oh really?' said Cora. It could be fun to play for a second team.

Beatrice nodded. 'You should sign up. You'd be a great asset to us.'

'Slow down, Cora,' her mam said. 'You want to join up with who now?'

'Carra ladies.' Cora was standing at the kitchen counter, bouncing on the balls of her feet as her mam stirred a casserole.

'But aren't you already playing with Ballin-tubber?'

'Yeah, but I won't be able to play with the boys forever. That's what Beatrice says. And until I'm old enough to play with Carnacon –'

'Hang on,' said her mam. 'Slow down. How many clubs are you going to be playing for?'

'Just Ballintubber and Carra for now,' replied Cora. 'And hopefully Carnacon in the future.'

'And school as well?'

'And school, yeah.'

Her mam shook her head, laughing. 'You'll wear yourself out, Cora.'

'I'll be grand, I promise!'

Her mam looked at her affectionately. 'You get your stubborn streak from me, anyway. But I don't know where you get your drive from.'

Cora wasn't sure either. All she knew was that she wanted to be the best that she could be, and she didn't see any point in setting limits on herself. The more chances she had to play football, the better.

'So, is that a yes?' she asked. 'I can join Carra?'

Her mother smiled. 'That's a yes.'

'Thanks, Mam!' Cora bounded over for a hug.

'But you have to organise your own lifts to training,' her mam said. 'And you're not to let football keep you from your homework or helping around the house. Deal?'

'Deal,' said Cora. She hoped she'd see Beatrice the next time she was in the field. She couldn't wait to tell her the good news.

CHAPTER 4

MOSNEY

Cora was a little bit nervous walking into her first training session for Carra. She had convinced Michelle to come along with her – partly because she knew Michelle would enjoy it, and partly so she wouldn't be walking in alone.

Within a few minutes, though, Cora realised she needn't have worried. The Carra girls were energetic and friendly, and they seemed to accept Cora and Michelle as their teammates right away. Cora didn't know many of them and would need to learn all their names, but once training started it was just like any other session: she got stuck in.

Before long, playing for Carra became part of Cora's routine. Beatrice gave her a lift most nights, or else Michelle's dad. Michelle's younger sister Sharon started coming to training too. Cora loved playing with the Ballintubber boys and would keep it up as long as possible, but it was exciting to be around a group of girls who were as mad about football as she was.

No one saw the Carra girls coming. They breezed through the Community Games competition, beating all challengers. Cora was their secret weapon. No one expected the small, skinny girl at corner-forward to be a threat – that was, until she started taking on the full backline and slotting goals past the keeper.

And just like that, they qualified for Mosney.

'What's Mosney?' Cora asked Eamonn, their trainer.

'It's a holiday camp in Meath,' he explained. 'They have chalets to sleep in, a fairground, restaurants, everything. And every summer, the national finals of the Community Games are held there. We'll be playing the best of the best.'

'Like an All-Ireland,' Cora said. She thought of the 1992 football All-Ireland the previous September, when Manus Boyle kicked nine points for Donegal to win them their first ever title.

He grinned. 'Exactly.'

They got a bus to Mosney together, the whole squad of them. The girls were giddy and excited to be away from home, talking about the fairground rides they were going to go on. They sang loads of songs like 'The Wheels on the Bus', 'The Rattlin' Bog' and 'The Green and Red of Mayo'. Cora sat at the back of the bus, singing and laughing with everyone else, but as she began to see signs for Mosney she grew quiet and moved up to the front of the bus, near Eamonn. It hit her suddenly that in a few days she could be playing in her first ever All-Ireland football final. She wanted to do justice to herself and her teammates. She wanted to have a stormer.

When they arrived at Mosney, there was a mad rush to claim bunks in the chalets. Cora managed to scramble onto a top bunk while Michelle grabbed the one beneath. Their first match wasn't until the following morning so they were let loose for the evening in the holiday camp. Cora had some pound coins jangling in her pocket, given to her by her parents and older siblings. She managed to spend most of her money in the arcade and on the bumper cars.

That night in her bunk, Cora closed her eyes, but try as she might, she couldn't fall asleep. She checked the time on her light-up digital watch: 12.45am. She stared at a crack in the ceiling and thought about the games to come. Beneath her, Michelle coughed.

Cora swung her head out over the edge of the bed. 'Are you awake?'

'Yeah,' came the whisper back. 'I can't sleep. I think I'm too nervous.'

'Me too,' said Cora. 'It might be all the Coke we drank earlier.'

Michelle giggled. 'Could be.'

'Let's just do what we usually do,' Cora said. 'You control the back, I'll score all round me.'

Michelle laughed again. 'Easy-peasy.'

'No bother to us.'

Cora lay back on her bunk again. The next thing she knew, it was morning.

The qualifying games passed in a kind of blur. It felt strange to be playing so many crucial games in such a short time. Cora felt as if she barely had time to catch her breath between them. But in another way, it was ideal. There wasn't enough time between matches for the nerves to creep in. There wasn't any time to doubt yourself. All you could think about was the next game, the next ball.

When they qualified for the final, they were almost too tired to celebrate.

Michelle hugged Cora at the full-time whistle. 'We're in an All-Ireland final! I knew we'd get there, I just knew it.'

Cora grinned back. She'd known it too.

The final was held on Sunday. Cora went to bed early the night before, though she would have loved another go on the bumpers. She had a quick stretch when she got up; her limbs were sore from the intense schedule of matches they'd had for the past few days. But her mind was ready. This was her first All-Ireland final, and she was not letting this chance slip through her fingers.

'Warm up, Cora. A cold footballer is no good to anyone.'

Her coach's voice broke through her daydream. Cora was standing on the 45 facing the goalposts, visualising all the scores she wanted to get in the game. It was raining, and there was an unseasonable chill in the air.

'I'm ready, Eamonn.' She turned and jogged back to her teammates, swinging her arms forwards and back. She watched the opposition warming up. They were a crowd from Kerry, and Cora could tell from their drills that they were a decent side. Carra would have a battle on their hands.

The game began well for them. The Carra forwards won a few early frees which Cora slotted over the bar. She was happy to get a few placed balls to settle herself. After ten minutes, she'd gotten a few scores from play as well. Michelle was having a stormer at centre-back and kept drilling the ball down Cora's wing – low and fast, the way she liked it. Cora's marker was much bigger and stronger than her but Cora was learning how to duck and weave, to use her opponent's force against her.

By half-time, Cora had kicked six points. The Kerry girls were strong, though, and Carra were only a point ahead.

'Let's go for broke now, girls,' Eamonn said. 'Cora, you're kicking points for sport but there's goals in you, I know it.'

The next ball Cora got, she turned her marker, breaking through the tackle. She was bearing down on goal when the corner-back came out of nowhere and mirrored her stride, blocking her path. Cora took the point; a part of her was impressed by the smart defending.

Just keep kicking them over, she told herself. *Your goal chance will come.*

But it never did. Michelle continued to deliver good ball; Cora, swarmed by defenders, continued to slot over points. The game was tense; there was only ever a point or two in it.

With five minutes to go, Michelle fell awkwardly

after jumping for a high ball. She landed on her arm. Even from up the field, Cora could see it was a nasty fall. Eamonn ran in to tend to her and moments later, Michelle walked off the field, holding her elbow.

'Brilliant game, Michelle!' Cora called after her as she walked off the pitch. 'We'll win it for you!' But inside, Cora was worried. Michelle had been controlling the game all day; without her, they were in trouble.

Just get it to me, Cora thought. *Just get the ball to me and I'll score a goal and we'll win.*

But the ball never came back to Cora. Five minutes later, Cora stood stock-still in disbelief as the referee blew his whistle three times. The Kerry girls around her started to shout and jump in the air. It didn't feel real. Cora turned and walked off the pitch. They had lost by a single point.

There were tears in the dressing room. But on the bus home, most of the girls seemed to have cheered up. They sat at the back and sang their songs, just like they had on the journey to Mosney. Only this time, Cora didn't join them. She sat on her own at the window, looking out at the rain.

After a while, she noticed someone sitting beside her: Beatrice.

'All right, Cora?' she asked gently.

Cora nodded.

'Do you want to talk about it? I know you must be disappointed.'

Cora turned to her. 'This wasn't the way it was supposed to happen,' she said, trying to hold back the tears. She wasn't just disappointed – she was sad, cross, frustrated and disappointed, all at once.

And then there was the regret. If only she'd taken on her marker more, gone for more goals instead of being content with points. If only she'd been more ruthless.

'You did brilliantly, Cora,' Beatrice told her. 'This is the first of many All-Irelands for you, okay? Remember that, and don't be so hard on yourself. And most importantly' – she looked Cora right in the eye – 'don't ever lose your enjoyment of football. Even on days like this, even on the worst days. If you can keep your enjoyment of the game, you'll go far.'

CHAPTER 5

CORA QUITS

In the following weeks, when Cora couldn't sleep, she'd sometimes find herself thinking about the Mosney final. The feeling of disappointment rose up fiercely in her, as if it had only happened yesterday.

Most of the adults around her acted as if it was no big deal. 'Hard luck,' they'd say, and sometimes even 'Sure wasn't it great to get that far?' That wasn't what Cora thought. To her, it was a terrible wrong that couldn't be made right. She felt as if no one understood.

She was no longer training with Carra – the season had finished up after Mosney – but she was still playing with Ballintubber. Then one night,

49

she just didn't go to training. She was supposed to organise a lift, but she didn't bother. That evening, it rained and rained and she stayed indoors racing Scalextric with her brother Brian. It felt like the easiest thing in the world.

Michelle rang her on the house phone afterwards. 'Where were you, Cora? I've never known you to miss training. Are you sick? Or were you stuck for a lift?'

Cora shook her head, then remembered that Michelle couldn't see her down the phone. 'I just didn't feel like it,' she said honestly.

Michelle didn't say anything for a moment, as if lost for words. 'Well ... do you want a lift on Saturday morning?'

'I'll let you know.'

When Saturday came, Cora didn't go to that session either. Her dad was moving the herd and she lent a hand by standing in gateways along the lane, making sure none of the cattle went astray. She barely even thought about football all morning.

That evening, the phone call didn't come from Michelle but from the Ballintubber coach, Seán. 'We'd love to see you back on the field, Cora. And remember, if you're not at training, I can't guarantee you a place on the team.'

'But I'm one of the best forwards you have,' Cora said. She wasn't saying it in a boastful way; it was just the truth, and Seán knew it.

'I know that, Cora, but it isn't fair to the lads who are training all the time if you're not showing up and then you waltz onto the team when there's a match. You have to put in the commitment.'

Cora sighed. She didn't want to go back training just yet, but she also didn't want to lose her place. 'I'll see you next Tuesday night, so.'

But the next night at training, she just couldn't get into it. Normally when she stepped on the football pitch, the rest of the world melted away. No school, no chores, no worries – just her and the ball. But not this time.

'Get into the game, Cora!' Seán shouted.

Cora shrugged. Usually the ball drew her like a magnet, but tonight she felt strangely tired, jogging around the place with no real purpose. It was like she was sleepwalking around the forwardline. When training finished, Cora spotted Beatrice watching from the sideline, her arms crossed. She'd seen the whole thing.

Beatrice fell into step with Cora as she jogged off the pitch. 'Not your usual self tonight, Cora.'

In the training game, Cora hadn't registered a single score. She'd kicked a few wides and gotten frustrated.

'Sure it's only a training game,' Cora said. 'It doesn't matter.'

'Of course it matters,' said Beatrice. 'You have to keep your own standards up, no one else is going to do it for you.'

'Like the standards we had in Mosney, you mean?' Cora fired back.

She walked up the steps to the stand without looking back. Beatrice didn't follow her.

Cora decided to quit for good. For a while she enjoyed the break. Her evenings were spent running around the farm with her brothers, daring each other to climb trees and jump off walls. If it was rainy, they'd stay indoors and play darts or board games. They were all competitive and sometimes their games disintegrated into rows, but that was part of the fun, too.

But then, something changed. It started like a nagging feeling in the back of her mind, a whisper that wouldn't go away. She'd catch sight of her yellow Mikasa gloves balled up in a drawer or her boots in the back kitchen, still muddy from the last training session. She'd feel the draw of them, but would always stop herself. After a while, it began to feel less like a whisper and more like a shout.

One sunny Saturday, she'd had enough. She got her bike from the shed and put her football in the basket. She cycled down to the community centre next to the school and found herself a big, blank wall. She started kicking.

No one made a fuss when Cora went back training, which was how she wanted it. Seán had her do a few extra laps at the start of her first session back, but otherwise he just seemed happy she was there. Some of the lads tackled her a bit harder than they usually did, but Cora didn't mind that; it would make her a better player.

'There's a spring back in your step,' Beatrice noted one evening, when she ran into Cora at the pitch. 'It's good to see.'

Cora just smiled. She'd fallen out with football for a while there, but now she was back and focused.

'And how are you getting on with the lads?' Beatrice asked. 'Are you enjoying training?'

'Loving it,' said Cora. And she meant it.

After a few weeks, Cora sensed that Beatrice was looking out for her, that she had taken her under her wing. Cora would often see her at the field after training, and Beatrice would always invite her for a kickaround if Cora was waiting for a lift home. She would ring the Staunton house and ask if Cora wanted to come to see a match somewhere in the county – both men's games and ladies, underage and adult. Cora always said yes. She loved watching matches, even if she sometimes felt frustrated that she couldn't run out on the pitch and join in.

Beatrice would do the driving, or else Jimmy

Corbett, the chairman of Carnacon. As far as Cora could see, they were both heavily involved with the Carnacon ladies football team. Jimmy was a quiet, modest man with ruddy cheeks and a ready smile, but Cora could tell there was a serious football brain behind it all. One evening, Beatrice, Jimmy and herself went to see a Minor match in Kiltimagh. They were playing Breaffy, and there was a close local rivalry between them. Cora marvelled at the height of the Minor lads, their bodies clashing in mid-air as they fought for the ball. Breaffy led for most of the second half, but Kiltimagh snatched it at the death with a well-taken goal. Cora jumped for joy on the sideline. It wasn't that she was supporting Kiltimagh – neither team meant anything to her – but it was such a confident, well-taken goal. The safe thing would have been to put it over the bar and draw the game, but the Kiltimagh forward wasn't interested in playing safe. Cora liked that.

On the way home, they stopped in a pub in Balla. Beatrice ordered a pint of stout and Jimmy, who was driving, had a Rock Shandy. Cora sat across the table from them on a low stool, drinking Coke and eating a packet of Taytos.

'Some goal,' said Beatrice.

Jimmy shook his head. 'Breaffy were robbed. A draw would've been a fair result.'

'Breaffy relaxed as the game was winding down,' said Beatrice. 'They left themselves open at the back.'

'That Kiltimagh corner-forward is lucky the goal went in,' said Jimmy. 'If he'd have missed it, he'd have been killed for not popping it over.'

'He wanted to win,' said Cora suddenly. 'He was never going to be happy to pop it over.'

Jimmy stared at Cora in amazement, as if he had forgotten she was there.

Beatrice smiled at Jimmy. 'She has that killer instinct, you see.'

Jimmy laughed and had a sup of his mineral. 'Just wait till you're ready to play for Carnacon, Cora. We'll have need of that killer instinct.'

'She's not far off being ready, I'd say,' said Beatrice with a smile.

Cora hid her grin by sipping on her Coke. Playing for her homeplace was her dream. She couldn't wait.

CHAPTER 6

CONFIRMATION

Jimmy and Beatrice were as good as their word. Before Cora knew it, she was lining out for the Carnacon Junior ladies football team. When he'd set up the club a few years previously, Jimmy had chosen green and red for the Carnacon jersey, and Cora felt a little thrill pulling on the Mayo county colours.

Once the jersey was on her, it went down to her knees.

Her older cousin Maria winked at her across the dressing room. 'Nice dress, Cora.'

'Thanks.' If she'd needed a reminder that she was out of her depth, this was it. These jerseys were designed for women, not skinny eleven-year-olds.

She tucked the jersey into her togs to make it fit a bit better.

They jogged out onto the pitch as a unit. When the referee called the captains for the toss, the team gathered in a huddle, arms around each other. Cora could feel how much this meant to all of them, to play for their homeplace. They jogged to their positions. Cora could see the full-back awaiting her: a tall, strong-looking woman in her twenties.

'Maria!' She called out to her cousin in the half line. Cora was suddenly full of doubt. But Maria was fourteen and had played adult games before; maybe she'd have some advice.

Maria jogged over and clapped her on the shoulder. 'All right, Cora?'

Cora glanced again at her marker behind her. 'What if … I can't …' She couldn't finish the sentence.

'Don't worry about her, Cora. All you have to worry about is the ball and the goalposts.'

Cora nodded. 'Okay.'

'And I'll be right here. I'll back you up a hundred percent, okay?'

'Okay,' Cora said again, with a bit more confidence this time.

'Good woman.' Maria clapped her on the shoulder again. 'You might be the smallest person on the pitch, but you've got the biggest talent. Don't forget that.'

The ball was thrown up. Cora tried to follow Maria's advice and forget about her marker, but it was easier said than done. She could tell that this full-back was more experienced than any she'd faced before, from her quick, firm handshake to the way she called out instructions to her teammates. The ball hadn't come to them yet but the full-back shadowed Cora constantly, always with a hand on her shoulder or arm – just letting Cora know she was there.

The first ball came, a high one kicked in from midfield. Cora braced herself to spring, but her marker had a good six inches on her. The full-back fielded it confidently from the air, took her three steps, and kicked it to her wing-back. Cora groaned. She had been hoping the full-back would fumble the ball, allowing her to win the break. Her marker wasn't just bigger and more experienced; she could play football, too.

'Next ball, Cora,' called Maria. She gave Cora a quick thumbs-up.

Cora prowled the 13-metre line over and back, hoping to shake off her marker, but the full-back kept following. A ball came up the wing, low this time. Cora sprinted as hard as she could to get to it, her marker close behind her. She gathered the ball and turned. She tried to side-step her marker and almost got past before the full-back pulled her down. The referee blew the whistle: free in.

'Brilliant stuff, Cora!' Maria shouted. 'Take her on every time!'

The free was converted and Cora felt a bit of satisfaction. It wasn't quite the same as scoring yourself, but knowing that your team got a score because of something you did was a pretty good feeling too.

She sprinted out to the next low ball that came in, but the full-back came with her and managed to reach in an arm to knock the ball away. Cora nearly growled in frustration.

'Stay patient, Cora,' Maria said quietly as she jogged by Cora. 'You'll get your chance.'

Just before half-time, a high ball landed on top of Maria. She won it and charged past her marker.

Cora saw her opportunity and began to back away towards the goals. The full-back was caught with a decision to make – either follow Cora, or close down the advancing Maria. She made her choice and went to Maria, who timed her pass perfectly. The ball looped over the full-back's head and landed in Cora's path. Cora grabbed it, soloed as far as the 13, and buried the ball low in the left corner.

'Wahoo!' Maria rushed over and jumped on her, celebrating like the soccer players on telly. 'Some goal!'

Cora grinned. She felt, finally, like she was off to a good start.

In the end, Cora scored 2-5. She was surprised when someone told her afterwards – she had no idea it had been that much. Sometimes it seemed as if she just needed to get that first score, and then the dam burst – the goals and points started coming thick and fast.

At the final whistle, the full-back turned to her and shook her hand. 'Good game. You're an absolute flyer.' And she walked off. Cora was too stunned to respond.

Jimmy came bounding over to her, a big smile on his face. 'Great performance, Cora! Do you know who that was, your marker? Bernie O'Neill. She plays full-back for the Mayo seniors!'

'Really?' She'd known the full-back was a good player, but she had no idea she was the best full-back in the county. Cora felt a surge of pride and a glimmer of hope. Playing for the Mayo senior team had long been her ambition; now it felt one step closer to being a reality.

That night, Cora lay on her back staring at the ceiling, unable to sleep. She was reliving the two goals in her mind, but she kept thinking about the end of the game as well, about what Bernie O'Neill had said to her. *I want to be like that when I'm older,* she thought. *I want to encourage young players. I want to be gracious, whether I've won or lost.* But most of all, she wanted to keep racking up big scores like she had today.

★

'I don't know, Mam.' Cora stared at her reflection in the mirror of the boutique in Castlebar. She was wearing a blue mini dress with a check pattern; there was a matching jacket to go over it.

'You look gorgeous, Cora.' Her mam stood back to admire her, hands on her hips. 'The colour brings out your eyes.'

'I don't know.' Cora examined herself in the mirror: the blue eyes, the blonde bob, the freckles, the wiry frame. It all looked familiar and normal – except for the dress.

'And it's not too girly,' her mam continued, reassuringly. 'No frills or anything. You'll be only fabulous making your Confirmation in this.'

Cora re-examined the outfit. It wasn't too bad, she supposed – actually, she looked fairly nice. It wasn't the worst dress she'd tried on today. It wasn't uncomfortable, and the length was okay – you could still see the grazes on her knees from when she fell in training. But she just didn't feel like herself in it.

'I'm just not sure if it's me, Mam,' she said eventually.

Her mam sighed. 'Well, you can't meet the

bishop in your jersey and togs! You'll have to find *something* to wear.'

Cora stepped back from the mirror and out of the changing rooms to walk around the shop floor. She spotted a few girls from her class, also out shopping with their mams for Confirmation, and gave them a wave. *Surely*, she thought, *there has to be an outfit in here that both me and my mam can be happy with*.

Then she spotted it in the corner on a mannequin: a crisp white blouse, a red waistcoat, and cool flared black trousers.

'Mam!' she called until her mother came over to her. 'What about a trouser suit?'

Her mam threw back her head and laughed. 'Trust you to find the only outfit in here that's not a dress or a skirt!' She walked over to the mannequin and had a closer look, a feel of the material. 'You know, this isn't too bad. Not too bad at all.'

The last few weeks of primary school were winding to a close, and Mr Ó Súilleabháin was getting a bit misty-eyed. He was taking the pupils outside for lessons when it was sunny and letting them watch videos when it was raining. He kept turning to sixth class, which included Cora and eight others, telling them how proud he was of them and asking them big philosophical questions about what they wanted to do with their lives.

'I know what your answer is, Cora,' he said, smiling, before she could even get out the words 'play football for Mayo'.

'And where are ye all heading for secondary?' he asked another day.

Nearly everyone said Balla, the local secondary school where Cora's older siblings, Sheena, Collette, Peter, Kathleen and Michael, had all gone. Cora just assumed that's where she'd go too.

'Balla,' she said, when it was her turn to answer.

Mr Ó Súilleabháin looked surprised. 'Not Ballinrobe?'

'No,' said Cora, confused.

'A word to the wise, Cora. Ballinrobe Community School has a very strong football culture.'

'Really?'

Mr Ó Súilleabháin nodded. 'Four senior school

All-Irelands in the last four years. Not bad, not bad at all …'

When she got home from school, Cora marched straight into the kitchen, where her parents were having a cup of tea. 'I want to go to Ballinrobe Community School,' she blurted.

'Hello to you too, Cora,' her dad said, with a wry grin.

'Sorry. Hi! How are ye? Can I go to Ballinrobe?'

'Wait wait wait.' Her mam took charge. 'What's all this about?'

'Ballinrobe is a really strong football school. That's where I want to go.'

'But what about Balla? Wouldn't you want your big sisters and brothers around to mind you?'

Cora shrugged. 'I'll be okay.'

Her dad smiled at her. 'You're a determined woman, I'll give you that.'

Her mam folded her arms. 'It's a bit late in the day, Cora. You're already registered for Balla. There's no guarantees that Ballinrobe will take you at this late stage.'

'Oh.' Cora's heart sank. She hadn't thought about details like that. She'd just been so excited at the idea of going to a school where football was centre-stage. She looked down at her shoes, her excitement deflating.

'But that doesn't mean we can't give it a try, does it?' her mam said.

Cora looked up at her mam. 'You mean it? You'll see if I can go to Ballinrobe?'

'Sure all we can do is ask,' said her mam, grinning.

Cora smiled broadly. 'Thanks a million!'

And she launched herself at her parents, throwing an arm around each of them.

CHAPTER 7

STARTING SECONDARY

On her third Monday at Ballinrobe Community School, Cora was starting to doubt her decision. This was partly due to her first class: double maths with Mr Plunkett.

'This is not a fair way to start a Monday,' Cora whispered to Grace, the girl at the desk next to her, who snickered.

Mr Plunkett seemed ancient to Cora – at *least* fifty – and was mumbling something about x and y. Every so often he'd ask a question and look for an answer ('Anyone? Anyone?'), but more often than not, he'd end up answering the question himself.

'This is torture,' Grace whispered back. 'I'm calling ChildLine.'

This sent Cora into a fit of giggles, which caught the attention of Mr Plunkett.

'What's so funny, Cora?'

Cora felt heat rushing to her cheeks. She hated being put on the spot in front of the whole class. 'Nothing, sir.'

'No, tell us. It's Monday morning. We could all use a cheering up.'

Cora tried very hard to maintain a serious face. She knew if she so much as glanced at Grace she'd burst out laughing again.

'I can't really say, sir,' said Cora.

'And why not?'

Cora thought her head would explode, she was going so red. 'It's private, sir.'

'Private? I see. A hundred lines for tomorrow, please, Cora: "I will not disrupt my classmates in double maths."'

'Ah, sir!'

'Never mind "Ah, sir". Just do the lines, okay?'

Cora folded her arms. She was going to have loads of homework tonight; there'd be hardly any time for playing outside.

'It's my fault, sir,' Grace said suddenly.

Cora stared at Grace in amazement. They barely knew each other; she couldn't believe that Grace was sticking up for her and taking the blame.

'What's that, Grace?' said Mr Plunkett.

'I was distracting Cora with stupid stories about the weekend, that's all,' said Grace. 'It's my fault, not hers.'

'Ah. In that case, Cora, forget the lines.'

Cora grinned. 'Okay, sir.'

'You can both report for detention tomorrow afternoon.'

Cora and Grace looked at each other in horror. Then they said in unison: *'Ah, sir!'*

She got in trouble with her parents, but the actual detention itself wasn't too bad. She and Grace had to behave themselves during, but they were able to chat before and after. Most of Cora's friends from primary school had gone to Balla, so she didn't know too many people at the new school. Grace was sound, though. It felt good to have a friend.

So far, Cora didn't much like secondary school.

She missed her old classmates and Mr Ó Súille-abháin. Back in primary, she'd known every single one of the hundred or so pupils by name. Here in Ballinrobe, she was one of nearly a thousand.

And she was just a snotty-nosed first year. The older students both fascinated and intimidated her: the girls with their rolled-up skirts and harsh laugh-ter, the boys with their gelled hair and loud, deep voices. At breaktime and lunchtime she was stuck in a stuffy, noisy social area instead of being out in the fresh air playing football, the way they did back in primary school.

Classes weren't much better. Cora liked some of them, in fairness – history and art, and science could be interesting sometimes – but most of the classes bored her to tears. She felt tense and frustrated, stuck at a tiny desk. She wasn't able to sit still but she wasn't allowed move around, either. Sometimes in those first few weeks, Cora thought she'd explode.

She was never more reliant on football. As soon as she got off the schoolbus she'd be out the back with a ball until her mam called her in for dinner and homework. She had training a few nights a week; herself and Michelle had recently been called up to the Mayo Under-14 squad, which was incredibly exciting and a chance to get to know girls from other clubs. If she hadn't had the excitement of football to balance out the boredom of school, she didn't know what she would have done.

Then, one day in October, it seemed things were looking up.

LADIES FOOTBALL TRIALS, read the poster on the noticeboard. Below, in smaller text, it gave the details for anyone who wanted to try out for the school senior team – the famous team that had won the four-in-a-row.

'Any interest?' Cora asked Grace, already knowing the answer. Grace was into reading and films and rollerblading, and she didn't know the first thing about the GAA. She would have struggled to name a single player on the Mayo senior men's team, whereas Cora knew them all off by heart. Somehow, though, they got on like a house on fire.

'Yeah, right,' said Grace. 'Do you want me to get flattened?'

'No, I just want someone to make me look good by comparison.'

Grace laughed. 'You don't need me for that. You'll run rings around them. Sure you're a Mayo Minor!'

'Under-14,' Cora corrected.

'Whatever. You'll be well able for it. Not a bother to ya.'

Cora smiled. What Grace had just said was a version of what she often said to herself in her own head – *You're well able, you're flying, you've got this.* Sometimes, though, it was nice to hear it from someone else.

'Thanks, Grace,' she said.

She was the only first year called up to the squad.

The day of the trials had been wet and mucky, the type of day that left brown and green stains all over her togs and bare knees. The bad conditions seemed to suit her, though – where everyone else was dropping the ball, she was controlling it; where everyone else was sliding and slipping, she skipped lightly over the ground. She scored two goals and a handful of points from play before the man in charge, Gerry, substituted her.

'We've seen enough of you,' he said, but he was smiling.

From then on, school took on a different vibe for Cora. No matter how boring class was, she always had football training to look forward to. They trained hard, two or three evenings a week and sometimes even in the mornings before class. Cora always dreaded the morning sessions – she'd be half-asleep in the cold and mist, and her breakfast would still be hopping around her stomach – but she always felt fantastic afterwards, ready to face the day.

The panel was loaded with talented players, and Cora felt a strong need to prove herself to them; to prove she was worth her place, even if she was only a first year. She set herself a target to rack up big scores in each game. Some of the older players began to take notice of her: the brilliant point-kicker Sinéad Costello; Denise Horan, who was sub goalie on the Mayo senior panel; and the Heffernan sisters Christina and Marcella. They started nodding to her when they passed her in the school corridors, which made Cora feel about a foot taller.

Training was *tough*. Some evenings after one of Gerry's sessions she'd go home, shower, and fall asleep on the couch with her dinner going cold in front of her. She thought she'd experienced a lot of challenges in her short career – playing with the lads in Ballintubber, playing junior for Carnacon, and playing at intercounty level with the Under-14s – but this was another step-up again. She thought maybe it had to do with them all being in school together and seeing each other every day – it made them push each other on, push themselves on. And the hyper-competitive atmosphere got results. The Ballinrobe CS forwardline understood each other like no team Cora had ever played on. They moved for each other, anticipated each other. It took a while for Cora to get the hang of it, to slot into place. But once she did, it felt like magic.

By spring, they were All-Ireland champions again, beating St Joseph's of Spanish Point in the final. *Five in a row! Five in a row!* the older girls sang on the bus on the way back home. Some of them had been on the team for all five.

'Some game today, Cora,' said Sinéad, sitting

down next to her. 'How does it feel?'

'It's just one in a row for me,' said Cora, 'but it still feels fantastic.'

Sinéad laughed. 'Get used to this feeling, Cora. Get addicted to it. The more you win, the more you want to win.'

Cora grinned. 'I could definitely get used to this.'

CHAPTER 8

THE CALL-UP

Cora was kept busy. Between all her various teams, she was playing or training seven nights a week. There was the Ballinrobe school team; the Mayo Under-14s; and there was Carnacon, for whom she played at Under-14, Under-16 Minor and Junior levels.

Jimmy checked in with her the odd time. 'Are you sure you're all right, Cora? Not feeling burnt out or anything?'

Cora vigorously shook her head and kept training. Sure, she got tired sometimes; there were nights when she was asleep almost before her head hit the pillow. But she always came away from training happy. She tried to remind herself of that fact on the evenings her limbs ached and she didn't feel like heading to the pitch.

'The most important training sessions are the ones you don't want to do,' Jimmy liked to tell them. 'That's when you find out if you're a winner or not.' Cora believed it.

They had a strong Under-14 team that year. Cora loved playing with the girls her own age – the girls she'd grown up with. It was a relief not to always be the youngest, smallest person on the pitch. And it was wonderful to look down the field and see Michelle patrolling the 45, knowing that if her friend got possession, she'd do her best to put it in Cora's path.

That summer, they reached the final of Féile na nGael, a national competition for Under-14 club teams that was hosted by a different county each year. It was in Mayo that summer, and all the Carnacon girls were determined to secure a win on home turf. 'Waterfalls' by TLC was all over the radio and this somehow became the squad's theme song. They'd scream out the lyrics at the back of buses to games; Cora liked the bit about having it your way or nothing at all.

The Féile na nGael final was held on a blazing day in June in MacHale Park in Castlebar, the home of Mayo GAA. It was the first time Cora had ever walked out on the pitch where she'd watched her heroes like Liam McHale and James Horan play. She had to stop herself from dropping to her knees on the hallowed turf. The surface of the pitch was perfect – none of the usual divots and dips she was used to working around – and even though the stands were mostly empty, the stadium gave her the sense of being on a stage.

She loved it.

Her enjoyment shone through her performance, Jimmy told her afterwards. She tucked away 1-8 as part of their win. Afterwards they sang victory songs in the dressing room with the cup, including 'Waterfalls' and 'There's Only One Carnacon'.

'Our first national title with our club!' Michelle said to her afterwards. 'Can you believe it?'

Cora put up both her hands for high-fives. 'The first of many!'

A few weekends after the Féile win, Jimmy rang the Staunton house. It wasn't unusual for him to ring Cora to arrange lifts for upcoming games or to discuss tactics, so when Collette handed her the phone, Cora thought it was just a routine call.

'I have something to ask you that I'd like you to consider carefully, Cora,' he began, and immediately she knew that this was about something big.

After she hung up, she walked into the living room in a daze.

'Is everything okay, Cora?' her mam asked.

'That was Jimmy on the phone,' Cora said, her voice shaky. 'He says … he says the Mayo senior ladies football management want me to join the panel.'

For a moment, there was a stunned silence.

Collette was the first to speak. 'But you're only thirteen! I mean, do they know you're only thirteen?'

Cora shrugged. 'Jimmy said they saw me in the schools All-Ireland and then in the Féile final and that's what decided them.'

'So Willie Joe wants you on his team, does he?' her father said, smiling. The legendary Willie Joe

Padden had been a Mayo senior footballer up until a few years ago; he was now one of the selectors for the ladies football panel. 'You can't very well turn down Willie Joe, I suppose.'

Her mam finally spoke. 'You'll have to think about this carefully, Cora.'

'What's there to think about?' The good news finally hit Cora, like an electric shock, and she danced around the room. 'I'm going to be a Mayo star!'

'Now Cora, we haven't said yes yet –'

'But this is all I've ever wanted, Mam.' Just as suddenly as she'd jumped around the place, Cora now sank heavily into an armchair. 'I have to take this opportunity. God knows when they'll ask me again.'

'But you're so young, Cora – you'll have loads of chances.'

'But Mam –'

'Cora, you're five foot nothing. You're what – seven stone?'

'I was well able to play with the boys, wasn't I?'

'This is different. At least the boys were the same age as you. Here, you'll be playing against grown women, women with strength and height and years of experience.'

'But I already play against grown women for Carnacon, remember?'

Her mam sighed. 'County is different, Cora. These women are the best of the best. And they're ambitious. They're not just playing for fun. They'd go through you for a shortcut.'

Cora felt her eyes grow hot. She blinked hard. She wasn't sure she could do this if her mam didn't support her.

'But Jimmy believes in me, Mam,' she said. 'And so do the Mayo managers – enough to give me a chance, anyway. Why can't you?'

Her mother's face softened. 'Hey – who's Cora Staunton's biggest fan?'

Cora smiled despite herself. 'Mary Staunton.'

'That's right. Don't you forget that! I believe in you a hundred percent, Cora. I've no doubt you're going to star for Mayo some day.'

Cora waited. She sensed there was a 'but' coming.

'But what's your rush?' her mam said. 'You're only thirteen, and you're already training seven days a week. What if you start training with the Mayo seniors and it's too much? What if it knocks your confidence and sets you back? Would you not be better off going when you're sixteen or seventeen, when you're a bit bigger and stronger?'

'It feels like the right time to me,' said Cora. She'd always been told she'd gotten her stubbornness from her mam, and now they were on opposite sides of an argument. She had no idea which of them would give in first.

'I only want to protect you, Cora,' said her mam. 'You have a special talent. I don't want it ruined for you by trying to do too much too soon.'

Cora sighed. 'I know you only want what's best for me, Mam. But how will I know if I'm able for it or not if I don't try?'

There was a long pause.

Finally, her mother smiled. 'I don't know where you got your determination,' she said wryly.

Cora grinned. 'So I can say yes?'

'You can say yes. But I want you to mind yourself, Cora, okay? If at any stage it feels too much for you, I want you to let me know. Deal?'

'Deal,' said Cora. She gave her mam a hug.

★

Cora made her senior debut for Mayo on a crisp October day in 1995. The game – a national league match against Monaghan – was actually her first time being with the squad; training wouldn't start up in earnest, she was told, until January or February.

She felt a little bit intimidated walking into the dressing room on her own. Then she spotted Christina and Marcella from Ballinrobe and went over to sit beside them.

'Fair play, Cora,' Christina said. 'Didn't realise you'd been called up as well.'

It turned out that a whole load of the Ballinrobe CS players had caught the attention of the Mayo management after their All-Ireland win; Sinéad had been called up, too. Cora was glad to see some familiar faces. The dressing room was buzzing with energy – many of the players seemed to have known each other for years, and the messing and in-jokes were flying thick and fast. Cora decided that the easiest thing was to laugh along, even if she didn't really know what the joke was about.

'Who's this?' A tall, boisterous woman turned around and looked at Cora. 'Jaysis, the gearbag is nearly as big as her. What's your name?'

'I'm Cora Staunton,' Cora said proudly. 'From Carnacon.'

'Nice to meet you, Cora Staunton from Carnacon. I'm Emma. Are you sure you're not the mascot now or anything?'

'No, I'm a forward,' said Cora hotly.

'One of the best forwards I've ever seen,' Christina said. 'I know she's only a squirt, but you should see what she can do with a football. Unreal.'

'Hey, I'm sitting right here!' Cora said. 'I'm not a squirt!'

Emma and Christina burst out laughing, and Cora realised that the whole dressing room was looking at them now.

'I can see you're not to be messed with, Cora,' Emma said. She held up her hand for a high-five. 'Welcome to the squad.'

Cora grinned and slapped her hand. A bit more relaxed now, she started putting on her socks and boots. It felt like she'd passed some kind of test.

Willie Joe came in and gave a short talk: 'We're giving a lot of new girls a chance today. Just go out and enjoy yourselves, girls – show us what ye can do.'

The team was announced and to Cora's amazement, she was picked at number 13. Sinéad, her Ballinrobe teammate, was also starting in the forwardline; she gave Cora a thumbs-up from the other side of the dressing room.

Cora pulled on the green and red jersey. Although it was – as usual – much too big for her, it felt just right. They ran from the dressing room to the pitch, making a sound that Cora loved – dozens of studs rattling off concrete.

Sinéad caught up to her. 'How are you feeling, Cora? It's okay to be nervous, you know.'

'Thanks. I'm fine, though.' It was true. In a strange way, Cora felt less under pressure than she did when playing for Carnacon or the Mayo Minors. On those teams she was expected to be the main scorer; if she had an off day, the team probably wouldn't win. Whereas here, no one had any expectations of her. She just had to do her best, that was all.

The game seemed to fly past. Thinking back on it later, certain things stuck out in her mind: the grass-stained white jersey of the Monaghan girl marking her; the commanding voice of Diane, Mayo's experienced centre-forward; the bored-looking cows in the field across the road from the pitch.

Cora had been eager to get a score early, to settle herself. The first ball she'd gotten, she'd run at her marker. The Monaghan girl was a tight back and had succeeded in forcing Cora onto her left foot. That was no problem to Cora; she slotted it over the bar, registering Mayo's first score. She could still remember the look of alarm on her marker's face as she realised *oh god, she can kick with both feet.*

Cora scored ten points from play in the end; six off her right, four off her left. Mayo still lost by three. If she was being honest, Cora barely even noticed the defeat. She was just elated that she'd played her first game for Mayo and played well. By the time she left the dressing room that evening, all of her new teammates had clapped her on the back.

CHAPTER 9

CORA GOES TO WORK

Cora arrived in one evening from training feeling tired, muddy and sore. She'd gotten a few thumps during the session and could already feel bruises swelling on her arms. In a way, she didn't mind about the bruises; it meant that her teammates didn't treat her any differently, despite the fact that she was much younger than most of them. *This is senior intercounty football*, she reminded herself. *You signed up for this.* Still, she was looking forward to dinner, a hot bath and an early night.

She threw her gearbag on the floor of the bedroom she shared with her older sister Kathleen. They got along well, even though they were completely different. You could even see it in their bedroom. Kathleen's side had a pretty floral bedspread and pictures of boybands taped on the walls, while Cora's had colourful striped bedsheets and posters of football All-Stars from over the years. Scattered on Kathleen's side were CDs, textbooks and makeup palettes, while Cora's side was shipshape, her football gear folded neatly in her dresser drawers.

She headed down to the kitchen to see what was for dinner. It looked like she'd arrived just in time: Kathleen was serving up pork chops.

Cora took a seat with her brothers and sisters. 'Where's Mam?'

Michael cleared his throat. 'Hospital.'

'Oh right,' said Cora. 'I didn't know she was working tonight. Where's Dad, so?'

Kathleen placed a dinner in front of Cora, and she tucked in.

'Gone with Mam,' said Michael. 'She's not working, Cora. She's sick.'

Cora's hands clenched her cutlery. Only now did she register how tense everyone looked, how worried.

'Is she okay?'

'Pneumonia, they think,' said Michael gently.

'They're keeping her in for tests. She'll be gone a few days.'

'But then she'll be okay,' said Cora. 'Right?'

'Hopefully,' said Kathleen, sitting down with her own dinner. 'You know Mam. Tough as nails.'

Cora nodded and tried to hold on to this comforting thought. But she had suddenly lost her appetite.

The house felt strange to Cora without her mother around. Her older sisters Collette and Kathleen kept things ticking over, while Peter and Michael looked after the farm. Cora and her brothers David and Brian – referred to as 'the smallies' by their older siblings, even though they were in their teens now – just tried to get on with their normal routines.

'I'm putting on a wash, lads, if ye've anything to go in?' Collette called up the stairs to them. 'Well, I say a wash – it's mostly Cora's muddy gear!'

'Sorry, Collette,' said Cora, laughing.

'C'mere and I'll show you how to use the machine. You'll need to know how to do this if you keep up the football.'

And so Cora started pitching in where she could, both on the farm and in the house. It was funny – she would've thought with their parents away, they all would've run wild, but it wasn't like that at all. Everything continued much the same as before.

That weekend, the three 'smallies' were brought to the hospital in Castlebar to visit their mother. Cora couldn't wait to see her mam – to tell her about how training was going or about Mr Plunkett's latest antics. But when they walked into the ward, she was shocked. Her mam was sitting up in bed, looking more pale and fragile than Cora had ever seen her. It had only been a few days since her mam had been at home, going about her day with her usual ferocious energy.

Her dad was sitting in the chair next to the bed. 'Hi lads,' he said, smiling.

'Hi, Mam,' said Cora, leaning in to give her a hug. Brian and David followed suit. 'How are you feeling?'

'Ah, I'm grand, thanks, Cora. Much ado about nothing, really.'

Cora saw her father give her mother a quick glance; sometimes it seemed as if they were communicating telepathically.

'I feel okay,' said her mother carefully, 'but they did find something in the tests. It turns out I have cancer.'

For a moment, Cora was frozen, unsure of how to respond. Her mother's words sounded serious, but her tone was light, almost as if she was talking about the weather.

'Are you going to die?' one of the boys asked, his voice small.

Her mother laughed. 'I've no intention of it, love.'

Eventually Cora found her voice. 'What happens next?'

'Your mam is going to have to go to Dublin for treatment,' her dad said gently. 'I won't lie to ye – it'll be a tough old road.'

'But we'll manage,' her mam added, with a sad sort of smile. 'We'll manage.'

★

One evening, her dad asked her to help him bring in the cows. Cora jumped at the chance. It wasn't often that she got to spend time with her dad one-on-one; usually at least one of her siblings was around. They walked down the lane together in their wellies, listening to the faint moo-ing of the cows in the distance. She could tell there was something on his mind.

'How are you feeling, Cora? About your mam being sick?'

If she was honest, the news hadn't quite sunk in yet. 'Okay, I suppose.'

'If you're fretting or worrying about it, you can always come talk to me. You know that, don't you?'

She nodded. 'Thanks, Dad.'

'This next year will be tough on us all. You kids are going to have to stick together and mind each other.'

'I know.'

'You're all going to have to grow up fast, too.' Her dad stopped and opened the gate. 'Do you remember my cousin Vincent?'

'The lad who owns the Carra Lodge?' Cora had stopped off in the pub a couple of times on the way home from matches. She'd met Vincent once or twice and liked him – a big, jolly bear of a man.

'He came over to me the other night when I was in for a drink. Said he's looking for a young one to work in the bar – collecting glasses, mopping down the counter, that sort of thing. What do you think?'

'Who, me?' said Cora.

Her dad laughed. 'Yes, you.'

Cora thought about it for a few moments: she'd have a bit of extra money, she'd learn a new skill, and she'd be able to eavesdrop on all the football chat from the lads on barstools.

'I'd love to,' she told her dad.

It was her first part-time job. She cycled to the Carra Lodge the next Sunday at noon and Vincent ran her through the basics of the job: how to work the till, use the bottle-opener, slice a lemon into perfect wedges. At the end of her shift, he let her pour a pint of Guinness from the tap. He took a theatrical slug from it when she'd finished.

'Perfect!' he declared.

The next Sunday, Cora worked a full eight-hour shift. She loved the work – how sociable and methodical it was, how she was never bored. The day would start out quiet; a few people out for a Sunday drive might come in for a coffee and a toasted sandwich, or some of the local teenagers would come in to play pool. But as the evening went on, it would become more and more lively – couples out for a few drinks with their friends or groups of lads after coming from a match, giving blow-by-blow accounts of the action.

There was a lot to take in, but she learned fast. After a month or so, Vincent gave her a set of keys, trusting her to open up on her own. The pay was decent and sometimes she even got tips.

'You can do this job anywhere in the world, Cora,' Vincent told her one Sunday. 'No matter where you end up when you're older. America, Australia, even Timbuktu.'

Cora laughed. 'I'm staying put in Carnacon.'

She had been coming to pubs with Jimmy and Beatrice after matches for years, and it felt so strange to be on the other side of the counter. Cora said this to Grace one day in school, and she burst out laughing.

'I feel the exact same way when I'm working in the newsagent. Behind the counter with all the sweets, it's mad!'

Cora felt like she was entering an exciting new time in her life – independent and capable, able to handle herself in the real world. She was fourteen. She was growing up.

CHAPTER 10

THE GREEN AND RED
OF MAYO

All the while, football was a constant in Cora's life. Playing for both club and county in several age groups meant that she was never without a game. At this stage, she approached all matches in the same way. It didn't matter if it was Under-16 for Carnacon or senior for Mayo – the important thing was that she went into the match focused and mentally ready. All the teams she played for had one thing in common: they relied on her to put up big scores.

She had been made captain of the Under-16 Mayo team, a role that she was honoured to be given but also found challenging. She felt under pressure to be inspiring, to give detailed pre-match pep talks in the dressing room. Underneath all her footballing swagger, she was still shy. She had no problem shouting encouragement and instructions to her teammates on the pitch, but speeches? It just wasn't her thing.

The Mayo senior men's team were in the All-Ireland final against Meath, and the county was buzzing. Red and green bunting was strung up on the streets of every town, and every house seemed to have a Mayo flag hung up outside it. Everyone felt sure that 1996 was Mayo's year. Liam McHale and James Horan were on fire, and Maurice Sheridan, a 21-year-old from Balla, was the championship's top scorer so far. Cora felt sure, too, that the silverware wouldn't be confined to the men. Mayo had a good Under-16 side that year, including Michelle and a few other girls from Carnacon, and the senior team were looking forward to a semi-final against Laois. If they won, they'd be into their first All-Ireland final ever. Cora was determined to make that happen.

Cora was working in the Carra Lodge the day the Mayo men played Meath in Croke Park. The pub was packed to the rafters and everyone was on their feet, straining to look at the tiny television that hung over the bar. The game was incredibly close, point for point. Cora could barely stand the tension.

It ended in a draw. A collective groan went up from the crowd.

'They'll have to do it all again, folks!' roared Vincent.

Cora got a bad feeling in her stomach. It had been over forty years since the Mayo men had won an All-Ireland; would their nerves be able to withstand a replay?

The bad feeling seemed to haunt her in the subsequent weeks. The Mayo Under-16 team that she captained were knocked out of the championship by Waterford; next, the Mayo Minor team on which she played a crucial role were beaten in the final, also by Waterford.

'If I never play a Waterford team again, it'll be too soon,' she said to Michelle afterwards, who laughed. Deep down, though, Cora admired them. Waterford had won four out of the last five senior All-Irelands, and clearly they were strong underage, too. Cora wondered what it must be like to win year after year, to have the expectation of success. What sort of standards did you need to set? What sort of mental preparation or team bonding did you need to be able to perform year in, year out? Maybe some day she'd find out, experience it for herself.

They had one chance left for redemption: the senior semi-final against Laois. It was the most high-profile game that Cora had ever been involved in, and her preparation was meticulous. She made sure she got eight or nine hours of sleep each night; she ate well, asking for second portions of potatoes and veg at dinner; she trained harder than she ever had before. Every night before she went to sleep, she played a video in her head of all the goals and points she was going to get, like a highlights reel on *The Sunday Game*.

Though she was used to her parents not being able to attend her matches, she really wanted them to be at this one. It wasn't going to happen, though. While her mam was in good enough form, considering, she didn't have much energy for travel. And her dad wasn't going to leave her mam on her own for the day.

'I'm sorry to be missing it, Cora,' her mam said. 'But don't worry. I'm going to see you win an All-Ireland final some day, I'm sure of it!'

On the morning of the game, her family waved her off with flags and headbands and plenty of fuss. Cora felt as ready as she'd ever be.

With fifteen minutes to go in the game, Cora was cruising. She'd racked up an impressive 1-10 so far, 1-5 of that from play. They were trailing Laois by two points, but no one was panicking; Mayo were getting the upper hand, and Cora was sure they'd get the scores they needed.

Her goal, early in the first half, had felt almost magical. The ball came in high and the corner-back ran in front of Cora and her marker to gather it. Somehow – she couldn't say how – Cora *knew* that the ball would bounce over the corner-back's head, and that it would come to her. Perhaps it was her years of experience coming into play; maybe it was the knowledge that the ground was still hard after the heatwave that summer and the ball was bouncing higher than normal. But it didn't feel like experience or a quick calculation. She just knew that the ball would bounce high over the back's head and that it would come to her, and come to her it did.

Time seemed to slow down. Cora took the ball in her hands and turned right, swivelling past her marker as if she wasn't there. Without looking, without thinking, she kicked the ball low and hard into the right corner of the net. Cora didn't actually see the green flag go up; her marker buried her as soon as she kicked the ball. But she didn't need to see the umpire's signal. She knew it was a goal before it even happened.

PHEEEEEP! The shrill blast of the whistle brought Cora back to the present. Diane had been brought down in the square and the referee's arms were outstretched, signalling a penalty. Cora's heart leapt. They needed to edge in front and here was the perfect chance on a platter.

Diane picked herself up off the ground and handed Cora the ball. 'No bother to you, Cora.'

Cora took the ball and placed it. She felt sure, confident. The goalie was tall and so would have a hard time getting down low. She'd put it in the left corner and they'd drive on from there. She took five steps back and waited for the ref's whistle, just like she'd practised. She could feel all eyes, all hopes on her.

She stepped up to the ball and struck it well, aiming for the corner with lots of backspin. The goalie was nowhere near it. And then it struck the post. Cora could hardly believe it as the ball rebounded into play and was cleared. She thought she'd picked her spot perfectly. It was only a matter of centimetres.

Cora was in a daze for the rest of the match, blood roaring in her ears. When the final whistle went, Laois were ahead by a point and into the All-Ireland senior final. As the Laois girls around her jumped and screamed in delight, Cora sank to the ground.

Sometimes the magic was on your side, and sometimes not. That was sport.

She was working when the men's replay between Mayo and Meath took place. Once again a crowd packed in to watch the small TV perched over the bar.

'This is like *déjà vu*, isn't it,' Vincent said as they worked side by side. 'I should've got in a big screen!'

Once again, it was unbearably close. The crowd grew more agitated as the game wore on. Cora stood rooted to the spot behind the bar. Vincent had told her to help herself to Coke and crisps but she didn't feel able to touch either of them. This was so much harder than playing yourself, she thought – wanting the team to win so badly, but not being able to do anything about it except shout at the telly.

Just after half-time, a row broke out near the goalmouth at Hill 16. It wasn't any sort of normal row – a few shoves here, a dig there. This row was *huge*. It seemed to Cora that every single player was involved, except maybe the Mayo keeper – and that was only because he was at the other end of the pitch! There were punches thrown, karate kicks, the works. The reaction from the crowd watching in the pub went from disapproval to concern to laughter; it was so bizarre that all you could do was laugh.

Vincent turned to her with a grin. 'You wouldn't

see the ladies at that, sure you wouldn't, Cora?'

'We have more sense,' she replied, and the punters on the barstools roared laughing.

Finally, the ref got control of the game again and called two players over: Mayo's Liam McHale and Meath's Colm Coyle.

'Sure how could he single those two fellas out?' Vincent cried. 'He'd have to send off the whole feckin' lot of 'em!'

McHale and Coyle were sent to the line. Cora hated to see McHale, one of her favourite players, walk off the pitch. She got that bad feeling in her stomach again.

Meath ran out winners by a single point. By the end of the game, the atmosphere in the pub was more like that of a funeral.

Cora had had her fill of losing: the Under-16s, the Minors, the seniors and now the men's. At times like this, Cora began to suspect that Mayo was cursed.

CHAPTER II

AT THE HOSPITAL

Sometimes Cora forgot that her mother was sick. No, it wasn't that exactly – it was more that her mother's illness quickly became part of normal life. Cora and her siblings all took on extra responsibilities: Collette and Kathleen did the cooking; Peter and Michael helped their dad on the farm; and Cora, David and Brian took care of other household chores like the laundry, dishwashing and hoovering. Sheena was living in Dublin, but came home as often as she could to help out. Between them they kept the show on the road, although Cora sometimes wondered how her mother had managed to do so much of this work on her own.

She was the same old Mam for the most part:

tough, funny, and always ready for a chat and a cuppa. The trips to hospital took it out of her, though, and she was pale and lacking in energy.

'I'm going mad here, Cora,' her mother confessed one night when Cora brought her a cup of tea. 'Having to sit still and rest! There's only so much telly you can watch.'

Cora understood; she hated having to sit still too. Luckily, her own life was incredibly busy, between school, working in the pub and football. Always football.

One day, her dad asked if she and Brian would like to go on a trip to Dublin.

'Definitely!' said Cora. 'How come we're going?'

'Your mam is starting the next phase of her treatment,' her dad said. 'But they can't do it in Castlebar, so she has to go to the Mater Hospital in Dublin.'

'Oh, okay.' Cora was pleased that her mam was getting a new type of treatment – maybe her form would improve and she wouldn't be so tired all the time. And she was excited to be going to Dublin. She'd only ever been in the capital a handful of times, usually for sporting reasons. She loved how everything was different there – the streets, the buildings, the throngs of people. In Carnacon if you met someone on the road, you probably knew them, but Dublin was full of fascinating strangers.

Herself and Brian were nearly giddy the morning they left for their mam's appointment, singing along to the radio in the backseat. When they stopped for petrol in Athlone, their dad bought them ice creams. Only when Cora noticed her mam's fingers drumming on the dashboard did she quiet down. Her mother was nervous, she realised.

When they got to Dublin, it was raining and the traffic was dreadful. Eventually, they made it to the hospital. Going through the automatic sliding doors was like entering into another world. The smell was what hit Cora first – a sterile, slightly sweet smell. There seemed to be no windows and the air was drier; Cora found herself breathing more rapidly. The fluorescent ceiling lights seemed too bright and too fuzzy at the same time. Even the smiling nurses looked eerie to Cora, in their matching blue outfits.

And then there were the patients. All of them seemed ancient and frail, even the ones who had kids Cora's age. They shuffled through the corridors in their pyjamas and gowns, some of them hooked up to drips that they walked alongside them like strange pets. Cora looked at her parents anxiously. Her mam didn't belong here with these worn-down sick people.

Cora's dad gave her and Brian money to spend in the hospital gift shop. They bought bars of Dairy Milk and cans of Coke and sat in the waiting room, flicking through copies of *Reader's Digest*, bored to tears.

When her parents came back, her mother's face was determined. 'I've to come back,' she explained. 'I'll be starting radiotherapy in James's next month. There'll be lots of trips to Dublin now, over the next while.'

'I don't have to come every time, do I?' said Brian.

Their mother laughed. 'Ye've both been very patient, in fairness to ye. I've a special treat for ye on the way home.'

'Are we stopping in McDonald's?' asked Brian.

'Yes. But there's something else, too. We're going to go see a certain landmark.'

Cora hadn't realised that the Mater was only a short walk from Croke Park. They walked over the canal, turned a corner, and Cora gasped. It looked incredible, a giant bowl plonked in the middle of the city. Almost like a spaceship, she thought – especially with the new, futuristic-looking Cusack Stand, which had only been built in the last couple of years.

Cora's mam came over to her and squeezed her hand. 'You'll be playing in there in a few years' time. I know it.'

Cora grinned. 'Thanks, Mam. And you'll be in the stands, roaring me on!'

'Oh, I will,' said her mother. 'I will.'

Cora might have imagined it, but she thought she saw tears in her mother's eyes.

In future years, when Cora looked back on the final months of her mother's illness, time got all jumbled up. Certain images stuck out to her: her mother's pill box, a plastic container with a section for every day of the week, which always seemed to be filled with tablets of different shapes, sizes and colours; a touch lamp that Kathleen bought her mam so that she'd be able to turn off the light without getting out of bed; a stack of books next to the bed that well-meaning neighbours brought but that her mam couldn't concentrate on because of the medication.

Normally Cora had a brilliant recall of games played and goals scored, but during her mam's illness, her memory got foggy. Maybe part of it was that she was so busy. As always, football took up most of her evenings. She continued to work at the Carra Lodge on weekends – sometimes even Friday nights now, if she didn't have a match and Vincent needed a hand.

Her mother went to Dublin for treatment every few weeks. Sometimes she was kept for days at a time. Cora worried that her mam would lose her lovely black hair, but she never did. The community in Carnacon did a bit of fundraising – a church collection, a table quiz in the Carra Lodge – and with the proceeds bought an all-expenses-paid trip to Lourdes for Cora's parents. Her mam had never been out of the country; Cora had never seen her so happy or touched.

Somehow, in the middle of all this, Cora did her

Junior Cert. She did okay, not brilliantly – unlike Grace, who got nearly all As. Grace tried to get Cora to go to a disco in Castlebar to celebrate, but Cora simply couldn't find the time. She and Grace were still friends, but Grace had started hanging around with a new group of girls who were into clothes and makeup and discos. It had never bothered Cora that she and Grace had different interests – Cora didn't get Grace's obsession with films any more than Grace got Cora's obsession with football. But now that Grace was into shopping and fashion magazines and wondering what some boy in school thought of her, Cora found it increasingly hard to connect with her. Grace's worries and problems seemed so small next to Cora's.

Sometime over the winter, Cora realised that her mam was getting worse, not better. It wasn't said out loud by anyone, but they all knew it. She could see it in her dad's eyes. She was in Transition Year, so she could afford to miss a bit of school. She stayed home more and more frequently, helping out around the house; sometimes her mam even needed help getting in and out of bed.

Her older sisters were gone from the house:

Sheena was working in Dublin, and Collette and Kathleen were in college there. They all did their bit to help at home when they could – when they were home for the weekend they put on load after load of washing and made huge dinners that could be divided up and put in the freezer.

But her sisters weren't there all the time, like Cora was, watching their mother getting weaker and weaker. Her dad and brothers busied themselves with farm work, leaving Cora to essentially run the household on her own. She was only fifteen. Sometimes she hated the unfairness of the world – why did she have to do all the housework, just because she was a girl? Why was her mam singled out to get this horrible illness?

Neighbours and friends started to flock around, to help, and that was when Cora really started to worry. Beatrice brought over a huge shepherd's pie and tried to engage Cora in football talk, but Cora couldn't concentrate. Vincent paid her a full day's wages even though she was only able to work a couple of hours. Maybe it was her imagination, but she even felt that her Carnacon teammates were going easier on her in training. *Don't feel sorry for me,* Cora wanted to yell. *Everything's fine. My mam is going to be fine.*

But deep down, Cora knew that wasn't true. She had the feeling of life being a high-speed train, the days going too fast for her liking. She knew what the next station was, but she wasn't ready for it. She didn't know if she'd ever be ready for it.

How could she even imagine life without her mam around?

CHAPTER 12

CORA'S MAM

The summer after Transition Year, Cora's mam was admitted to Mayo General Hospital in Castlebar – the hospital where she'd worked for years – and was kept there. Cora expected there to be a call that her mam would be coming home soon, but it never came.

Instead there was a different sort of call. The doctors rang the house and told her dad that there wasn't much time left. Immediately, they all made their way to the hospital, her sisters making the long drive from Dublin.

They spent the next few days camped out in their mother's hospital room and in the corridor outside: all eight Staunton kids, Cora's dad, plus a rotating cast of aunts, uncles, cousins, friends, doctors and nurses. They slept in armchairs. They forgot to eat. When they did go out for some food, they did it in shifts, so that there would always be someone there with her mam.

Her mother slept a lot. She was weaker than Cora had ever seen her, but at least she didn't seem to be in any pain.

On the third night, Cora and her siblings went out for some chips. It was late on a Friday night, so the queue was massive. Cora was hungry and bored.

'Here, Peter, let me play with your mobile.'

Her older brother Peter was the only one of them who had a mobile phone. At first, they teased him mercilessly for being flash, but now they all envied him his cool gadget. Cora, in particular, loved playing the Snake game that came with the phone: you controlled a long black line that travelled around the green screen, eating up any dots that came in its path. With every dot, though, the snake became longer, and if it touched off the edge of the screen it died. Cora was good at it; she'd set the high score on Peter's phone.

Halfway through her game of Snake, the phone started ringing. She handed it to Peter straightaway. She knew what the call meant.

Peter listened for a moment, nodded and hung up. 'We've to go back to the hospital, lads.'

They crowded into the hospital room as their mam's breaths became shallower and shallower. The room was very quiet. Her dad held her mam's hand; in his other hand was a set of rosary beads. He worked through them quietly.

Her mam's breath was laboured but still rhythmic; Cora became lost in its rise and fall. And then, once, her mother didn't inhale, and they all looked at each other, and they knew it was over.

Her dad bowed his head and cried. Cora had never seen him cry before. Kathleen put an arm around Cora and held her fiercely, fighting her own tears. Cora's mind was racing. *It's a mistake*, she wanted to say. *This isn't real.*

Doctors came and said official-sounding things. Nurses said sympathetic things. Peter drove them home while her dad stayed at the hospital to take care of her mother's affairs. It was six in the morning by the time Cora crawled into her own bed.

She pulled the covers over her head and, for the first time in weeks, she cried.

Later they would say that the funeral had been lovely, a fitting tribute to her mother, but at the time Cora had just tried to keep breathing. Most of the funeral went over her head.

She remembered saying goodbye in the funeral home. She kissed her mam's forehead and, in her mind, said 'goodbye, Mam'. She remembered the house being full of people and food and chairs being lined up in the hallway to accommodate everyone. She remembered Beatrice sitting with her, talking to her, as she cried. She remembered her team-mates hugging her, and thinking how strange it was to see them in good clothes as opposed to football gear. They were probably thinking the same about her.

She remembered Vincent putting his arm around her at the graveside. She remembered trying to comfort her dad but not knowing how. She remembered feeling closer to her siblings than ever before, because they were all in it together; they were the only ones who could really understand.

Any time she was on her own over the few days, Cora either cried or felt so angry she wanted to punch the wall. So she stuck with people as much as she could. Friends, neighbours, family. If there was someone else there, she could bear the pain. On her own, she went to pieces.

Three days after the funeral, Jimmy rang her. 'Are you available for the match tonight, Cora?'

Carnacon were due to play championship that night. She'd forgotten all about it.

'I don't know, Jimmy,' she said. 'I don't feel great.'

It wasn't just the grief. Cora hadn't been sleeping, and over the few days of the funeral, she'd either been forgetting to eat or else eating complete rubbish. She'd even snuck a glass of brandy when her dad wasn't looking. She didn't like the taste, but it warmed her belly and quietened the noise in her head.

'It'll do you good,' Jimmy said. 'Football is what

you do best, Cora. You love the game. And at times like this, it's really important to remind ourselves of the good things in life.'

'I really don't feel like it, Jimmy.'

'Your club needs you. We're really stuck for numbers –'

'I said I don't feel like it, Jimmy!' Cora hung up. For a moment, she stared at the phone in disbelief. She had never raised her voice to Jimmy before. She had certainly never hung up on him mid-conversation. But she was a different person now. These last few days, weeks, months had changed her.

She went to her room and lay on her back on the bed. She thought about her club going out to play championship that evening and found she could not care less. Before, she would have circled the fixture in her calendar and looked forward to it for weeks. Now it meant nothing.

She started to think, then, about the amount of football she had played over the last ten years. Every evening, out the back or over at training. Neglecting homework, neglecting jobs around the house to cram in more football. How many points had she kicked over the bar in the last decade, and how many times had she hugged her mother? She knew the numbers couldn't even compare.

Infinite days of football stretched out in front of her, but there would be no more time with her mam. No more hugs. No more cups of tea. No more chats at the kitchen table. No more times when her mam would be 'giving out' to her, but Cora would catch the glint in her eye or the quirk at the side of her mouth that meant she was trying not to smile. There would be no more of that.

Oh, but there'd be all the time in the world for football, she thought bitterly. Suddenly, Cora was angry at football, for taking her away from the most important person in the world. For a moment, she was even angry at herself.

CHAPTER 13

CORA FINDS HER
WAY BACK

Somehow, as a family, they struggled on. They had no choice, Cora supposed. Kathleen took a year out of college to move back to Mayo and look after the household. Cora felt bad that Kathleen had to put her studies on hold, but she was also grateful to have her big sister back.

The absence of her mother felt like a huge, scary void that could never be filled. No amount of friends, no amount of homework, no amount of football could dislodge the pain and loneliness she felt.

The best she could hope for, she discovered, was numbness. One evening when she took a football down to the community centre to have a half-hearted kickabout, a guy she recognised from school offered her a can from a plastic bag. She looked at the label: a cheap supermarket brand of beer. She shrugged and took a sup. It tasted sudsy and of old socks, but the more she drank, the fuzzier her head felt and the farther away her pain and loneliness seemed.

She started going to the community centre some evenings to drink beer and smoke a few cigarettes with the teenagers who hung around there. She knew she was too young to be drinking and smoking, but reasoned she was also too young to be without her mother. It wasn't great behaviour, but nothing really mattered now that her mam was gone, so what harm?

At school, she hung around with the same crowd at break and lunch. They'd sit on the wall at the back of the school yard, making fun of the teachers. Grace couldn't understand why Cora didn't want to hang out with her anymore. The truth was that Cora couldn't stand the pity she saw in Grace's face every time they spoke. Grace was trying to be nice, Cora knew, but there was no way she could understand what Cora was going through. It felt easier to drift away and let the friendship lapse.

One evening, Cora was sitting on the grass outside the community centre, finishing a lukewarm can, when a familiar car drove up. She put the empty can into a plastic bag and got to her feet.

Beatrice got out of the car and opened the boot, taking out a couple of footballs. She kicked them over to the playing pitch. Beatrice no longer played for Carnacon – she was purely a mentor now – but she still liked to have a kickaround every now and then. Cora knew that Beatrice had seen her so there was no point in hiding. She walked over.

'Hi Beatrice.'

'Hi Cora,' said Beatrice. 'Long time, no see.'

Cora didn't know what to say. 'Don't often see you around here,' she said eventually.

'There's a match down at the club, so I said I'd come here,' said Beatrice. 'Will you kick the ball back to me?'

Cora shrugged. 'Sure why not.'

She stood behind the goals in the shade of the big oak tree and caught the points that Beatrice slotted over. Despite the fact that she hadn't played in a few years, Cora noticed, Beatrice was still a very accurate kicker.

'You should come out of retirement,' Cora called out to her, grinning.

'I could say the same thing to you!' Beatrice responded.

Cora cursed mentally: she'd walked into that one!

Beatrice jogged in to the endline. 'I need a break. Why don't you have a go?'

Reluctantly, Cora switched places with Beatrice. She lined up the three balls on the 45 and swept them cleanly over, one by one.

'Nice one!' Beatrice called, kicking them out to her again.

Cora repeated the exercise. It was soothing in a way, she thought. When she was placing the ball, lining up the shot and kicking it, she wasn't thinking about anything else. Not about school, not about how angry she felt – not even about her mam.

'Great stuff, Cora!' Beatrice shouted as she kicked over another point.

Cora stayed there until dusk, practising her frees. By the time she went home, she'd promised Beatrice that she'd come back training for Carnacon. Her team needed her, Beatrice said. Cora now realised that she needed them, too.

Cora hoped to duck in to the next training session unnoticed, no fuss, but as soon as she stepped into the dressing room, her teammates started applauding.

'Ah lads,' she said when it died down. 'There's no need for that craic.'

'We missed you, you big eejit!' Michelle yelled, throwing her football gloves across the room at Cora. Then her cousin Maria dumped the contents of a water bottle on Cora's head and all hell broke loose. Cora laughed until she cried. She was back.

Jimmy called her aside after training. Cora wanted to speak first, to apologise for what she'd said on the phone, but Jimmy held up his hand.

'I've a favour to ask you. Will you be captain?'

Cora shook her head. 'No way. I've already missed

one championship match. I don't deserve it.'

Jimmy shrugged. 'You're their leader, Cora. No matter what, you're their leader.'

There was something special about Carnacon that year; they simply weren't going to let anyone else stop them. There was a calmness in the dressing room before games that Cora had never seen before. The club had been in existence for five years now, and Cora's generation of players were coming into their own.

For the first time ever they got to the county final against their closest rivals, their neighbours Hollymount, who were going for four in a row. Tempers often flared when the teams met, and Cora in particular came in for rough treatment.

'Oh my god, it's the great Cora Staunton!' her marker said in a high, fake voice at the start of the game. She dug her elbow hard into Cora's back. 'I'm not worthy!'

Cora just laughed. 'You're right, you're not.' That shut her up fairly fast!

Since coming back to training, Cora had become a different sort of player. There was steel in her now. She was taller and stronger, and well able to physically compete with the backs she encountered. Before, she would always have been friendly towards her marker; she took it personally if they jeered her or called her names. Before, she would have worried about what was written about her in the newspapers, or what referees and mentors and opposition players thought of her. Not anymore. She had a new perspective now; she knew what was important and what wasn't worth worrying about. She knew that her family, friends and teammates had her back, and that was all that mattered. She knew that you couldn't please everyone. Losing her mam had changed her, but she was stronger now.

They won the final by an impressive margin, as Cora knew they would. Accepting the cup in the evening sunshine, with her teammates and the people of Carnacon gathered around her, reminded her of why she loved football, why all the work and sacrifice was worth it.

She was called on to say a few words. After thanking her teammates, the management team and the referee, Cora turned to the supporters. 'I want to thank the people of Carnacon for always believing in us and supporting us. We all have a brilliant support system around us and we've ye to thank for that. Unfortunately, some of our staunchest supporters through the years can't be with us today. But I know they're with us in spirit.'

She met her dad's eyes in the crowd, and he smiled at her. For a second, Cora felt her throat tighten and thought she was going to cry. She coughed and tried to steady herself.

'Finally,' she shouted, 'three cheers for Hollymount! Hip hip!'

And the crowd roared back: 'Hooray!'

CHAPTER 14

CRAZY DAYS

Though she loved being back playing with Carnacon, Cora didn't feel ready to return to the Mayo setup until the following January. She knew the focus and dedication that intercounty demanded, and in the wake of her mam's death, she wasn't mentally in the right place to handle the challenges.

Six months on, maybe she still wasn't ready – but she was willing to find out. Just like with Carnacon, her Mayo teammates welcomed her back with open arms. There was a new coach involved, an amiable red-headed guy called Finbar Egan. 'He's tougher than he looks,' Diane said in the dressing room, and she was proven right.

Finbar's speciality was called an Up and Down. 'Ye'll enjoy this, girls,' he said as he introduced the drill. He got them to line up on the endline holding hands – all thirty of them – and then sprint to the opposite endline. 'Either ye all make it as a unit, or none of ye do!' Finbar bellowed. That first night back training, they did twenty Up and Downs. Two girls even threw up their dinners! But they kept going as a team and got through it.

Cora had known a lot of her Mayo teammates for years – the likes of Christina, Marcella, Denise and Sinéad from her school team and of course Michelle, Martha and Maria, who played for Carnacon. But she found it strange, sometimes, meeting girls from rival clubs – girls who had been her opponents on the pitch – and suddenly having to think of them as her teammates.

There was one girl in particular who Cora knew only as Crazy. From the team sheets, Cora knew that her real name was Yvonne Byrne, but she had never heard anyone call her 'Yvonne' in real life. Cora recognised Crazy from the county final against Hollymount: at centre-back, she'd caused a fair amount of hassle by cutting off some of the supply of ball to Cora at full-forward.

'Why do they call her Crazy?' she whispered to Sinéad before training one night.

'I think it's because she once punched a girl in the face over a disputed line ball. Knocked her out cold.'

'*Really*?' said Cora, scandalised.

Sinéad nodded, her face deadly serious. 'Oh, and another time, she bit an opposition player on the ankle in a ruck. The girl had to get stitches and everything.'

'Jeepers,' said Cora. 'You wouldn't think it to look at her.'

That very night, Cora ended up marking Crazy in a training session. She couldn't help but sneak glances at her from the corner of her eye.

'What is it?' Crazy asked at one stage.

'How do you mean?' Cora responded.

'You're looking at me like I'm …'

'Crazy?' Cora suggested.

Crazy laughed. 'Well, yeah.'

'Sinéad was telling me how you got your name,' Cora explained.

Crazy shrugged. 'It's because I'm mad craic, basically.'

'No, she was telling me about the girl you punched on the playing field. Oh, and the time you bit someone.' It was only when Cora said it out loud that she realised how ridiculous it sounded.

'Sinéad said that?' Crazy went quiet for a moment, and then started to laugh. She laughed until she cried. *'And you believed her!'*

Cora could feel her cheeks heating up. 'No, I knew she was messing,' she lied.

'Here, Sinéad!' Crazy shouted. 'Cora believed everything you told her about me! Hook, line and sinker!'

The sound of Sinéad's laughter floated over on the evening breeze.

'God, you're fierce gullible, Cora,' said Crazy, patting her on the back.

'I'm not, I swear!' Cora protested.

'Ah, don't worry about it. You wouldn't be the first one Sinéad has codded. Besides,' Crazy added, 'I only bite people when I'm *really* mad.'

Then it was Cora's turn to crack up.

They drew Meath for the All-Ireland semi-final.
Meath were a strong team, but the way Mayo were
going in training, Cora felt certain they could pull
off an upset. Their training games were getting
ferociously competitive. They were a young squad,
bursting with talent, and no one's place on the team
was safe.

The day before the semi-final, they piled onto a
bus in Castlebar and began the long winding journey east, picking up players along the way. Everyone
cheered when Claire Egan, a talented midfielder,
boarded the bus. Claire had a fixture clash that weekend; she was also due to play soccer with the Irish
Under-18 team, and no one had been sure which
team she would choose. Cora was grateful that
Mayo football had won out this time, but she didn't
envy Claire her dilemma. She saw it all the time –
girls who were talented at other sports, be it soccer,
rugby, basketball or camogie, having to choose one
sport over another. Cora had always enjoyed playing
other sports, but her heart was in the GAA. It made
life simpler.

She was happy, too, that they were doing most of
the travelling the day before the game, stopping for

the night in Maynooth, County Kildare. Cora sometimes found the long bus journeys before matches nerve-wracking, especially if it was a bumpy ride with lots of winding roads and potholes. Her stomach would start churning, which would add to her pre-match anxiety. Travelling the day before gave them a bit of breathing space.

Cora awoke the day of the match feeling ready for anything. The game was in Parnell Park in Dublin, and when they arrived an RTÉ crew was setting up outside the grounds. For the first time ever, the All-Ireland ladies football semi-finals were going to be broadcast live. Cora had never played a match that was televised before.

Crazy nudged her. 'It'd be great to watch the match back later, wouldn't it?'

Cora nodded. They both knew the only way they'd be able to stand watching it back was if they won.

At half-time, they were four points down. Normally, Cora would be concerned about a gap like this, but there was no fear in the dressing room. Heading back out onto the pitch, Cora knew that they'd pull back the margin, point by point. Sinéad got the first one. Their captain, Diane, got the second. Orla got the third. And with ten minutes to go, Cora grabbed the ball on the edge of the square and smashed it into the back of the net.

When the final whistle went, Cora leapt into the air with glee. For the first time ever, the Mayo senior ladies football team were headed to Croke Park!

They went hell for leather at the next few training sessions. Everyone wanted a place on the starting fifteen in the All-Ireland final against Waterford. As for Cora, she wanted to prove that she was the fastest, hungriest, most ruthless forward on the squad. She fought like mad for every ball, and tonight's session – on a glorious sunny evening a week before the final – was no exception.

A low ball came bouncing down the wing. Cora tore after it, making a beeline, eyes only on the ball.

CRACK.

She hit the grass. A white-hot bolt of pain shot up her shoulder. Claire was sprawled on the ground next to her. They'd collided, she realised; they'd both gone for the same ball.

'Are you okay, Cora?' Claire asked. Her brow was furrowed with concern.

'I'll be grand,' said Cora, wincing through the pain. But she could tell from the look on Claire's face – and the faces of the other players and Finbar, now gathering around – that she was not grand.

Her cousin Maria drove her to the hospital in Castlebar where her mother had died. She was told by a doctor that her collarbone had snapped, but she was sent for an X-ray anyway. It was only while on the table getting X-rayed that she allowed herself to think it: she wouldn't be able to play next Sunday. Mayo's first ever All-Ireland final, and she would miss it. She could barely move without wincing in pain; how would she ever get through a game of football?

Right there on her back, with the X-ray machine hovering over her, Cora began to cry.

CHAPTER 15

THE ALL-IRELAND

Cora was sitting on her bed, staring into space, when she heard a knocking on her bedroom door. 'Go away!' she roared.

'It's just me, Cora.' She heard her dad's gentle voice. 'I was just wondering if you'd like some dinner?'

'I'm not hungry.' She knew she wasn't being fair to her dad, but she couldn't help it. Inside she was a tangle of raw emotions. She glared at the sling on her arm, a constant reminder of her injury. She hadn't felt this angry and confused since – well, since her mam died.

'Grand so,' said her dad. He paused. 'Umm … there's someone else here who'd like to talk to you.'

'Hey, Cora.' It was Beatrice, her voice slightly

muffled through the door. 'Okay if I come in?'

At the sound of Beatrice's voice, Cora found herself calming down a bit. 'Fine,' she said, 'but only for a little while.'

Cora sat up a bit straighter as Beatrice came into the room. Unlike the looks of pity and concern that she'd been getting from everyone else, Beatrice was smiling, as if this was just an ordinary meeting between them.

'How's the shoulder?' she asked, nodding at the sling.

'Useless.'

'I mean, how is it feeling?'

'Useless,' Cora repeated.

'Any pain?'

'A bit,' Cora grumbled. 'That's the least of my problems, to be honest.'

'I know.' Beatrice sat down on Cora's desk chair. 'It's an awful dose, Cora. Both for Mayo and for you personally. You've been terribly unlucky.'

Cora ducked her head. It felt good to have someone acknowledge what she'd been thinking, over and over, for the past few days. She felt she could say things to Beatrice that she couldn't say to anyone else close to her. Beatrice wouldn't judge her or get upset.

'The thing is,' Cora said, 'I've felt for a while that I'm due some good luck. You know? Since Mam died. I felt like I deserved something good to happen. I thought this was it – the All-Ireland final! And I worked so hard for it …' Cora felt her throat closing up.

'That's very understandable,' said Beatrice quietly. 'You're due some good luck, there's no doubt about it.'

'I want to play in Croke Park.'

'You will,' said Beatrice, with certainty in her voice. 'You're still only seventeen, Cora. There's years left in you. Years and years.'

'But what if this was my only chance?' Cora said. 'What if we never get back into a final? What if Mayo's cursed?'

Beatrice seemed to find this hilarious, but Cora was deadly serious.

'Maybe Mayo has been cursed in the past,' said Beatrice eventually. 'But if so, I think this bunch of girls is going to be the team that breaks it. They'll do it for you, Cora.'

'I hope you're right.'

'I know I'm right. And if somehow they don't win it for you? I'll murder the lot of them.'

Almost despite herself, Cora laughed. 'Ah, Beatrice, come off it!'

'I'm serious. With my bare hands.' She held up her fists threateningly. Cora laughed harder, then winced; laughing made her shoulder hurt.

They talked for another while and Cora found herself feeling a little bit calmer. Less torn apart inside.

'You're still a vital part of the group,' Beatrice said, just before she left. 'Remember that. They need you with them.'

Their plan for the weekend of the final was the same as the Meath game: stay in Maynooth overnight before driving into Dublin on the Sunday morning. Boarding the bus in Castlebar was a much different experience this time. The girls were quieter, more nervous, almost gloomy. Claire looked like she hadn't eaten or slept in a week.

'We're all heartbroken for you, Cora,' said the captain, Diane. 'But we're even more determined now to win it. We'll be thinking of you out there.'

'Thanks, Diane. I know ye will.' Cora had to try to be positive, both for herself and for the girls around her. Crazy made the bus journey feel shorter, messing and making her laugh, distracting her from her disappointment.

Cora and her cousin Maria were settling down for the night in their shared room when Finbar knocked on the door. He asked them if they were all set for the next day, then out of nowhere, he said: 'You're starting tomorrow, Cora.'

Cora just stared at him. She thought he was joking, only it wasn't very funny.

'Come off it, Finbar. I can't start.'

'Correction – you can't *play*. But you can tog out, and walk behind the Artane Band, and line out for your first All-Ireland final in Croke Park. We'll substitute you after a minute or so. Well, what do you think?'

Maria was smiling, delighted for her, but Cora was still in shock.

'I think you're mad, Finbar.'

He laughed. 'Well, are you interested, or …?'

'Of course I'm interested!' Cora's shock started to give way to delight. She had been dreading the next day, sitting in the dugout in her tracksuit, envying all the girls out on the pitch. This wasn't everything, but it was *something*. But would it work?

She thought for a moment. 'What if … what if I line out and the corner-back does something? Hits me a dig or shoves me to the ground? I could end up doing even more damage.'

Finbar shook his head; he'd thought of everything. 'I've already spoken to the Waterford manager. I explained the situation to him and he promised me that no one will touch you. "As long as this isn't all an elaborate plan to get a goal in the first minute" were his exact words.'

Maria laughed. 'Can you imagine? Let's just put Cora on the edge of the square and get the ball to her as quick as possible. I'd say she'd be well able to score a goal, broken collarbone and all.'

'There'll be no funny business, now,' Finbar said, grinning. 'You'll be gone in under a minute. What do you say?'

Cora smiled. 'Sounds good to me.'

★

Cora woke up on the day of the All–Ireland with a sense of hope and excitement, rather than the dread she'd been expecting. Somehow, the chance to walk out on the turf with her teammates made all the difference.

In the dressing room she was handed the number 13 jersey. She grinned at Michelle across the room, remembering the very first competitive match they'd played with the Ballintubber boys, years ago now. She'd been handed number 13 that day too. *Unlucky thirteen*, Michelle had said, messing. Today, the jersey marked her out as unlucky – but for the first time in ages, Cora felt confident that her luck would soon change. She would make sure of it.

As they stood in the tunnel waiting to take to the field, she slipped off her sling. The Waterford play-ers all knew that she was injured, but she still didn't want to show any obvious signs of weakness. Water-ford were the reigning champions and had broken Cora's heart at different times over the years, both at underage and senior. She would have loved to be able to take them on.

Cora jogged onto the pitch, wincing a little as the impact from the ground shot up through her shoulder. She looked up at the stands at fifteen thousand fans cheering and waving flags. She had never been part of a game with such a big attendance before. The noise they made sent a chill down her spine.

She was finally here, on the pitch she'd daydreamed about as a girl. She knelt down and ran her palm across the grass. The sod was perfect. She stood up again and turned around, taking in the stadium from every angle. Croke Park had the effect of making you feel tiny and like a giant, both at the same time. Soon it was time for them to walk in the parade behind the Artane Band. Cora had watched this moment on TV countless times. It felt surreal that she was finally part of it.

While the national anthem played, the Mayo girls stood in a line on the 45, their arms around each other. Cora looked down the line, saw the concentration etched into every face. They were ready. Even Cora had never felt so psyched up for a game in her life! But she would have to give way soon.

She jogged out to her place, her injured arm hanging awkwardly, and shook hands with her marker. In the Waterford girl's eyes, she saw the same look of determination that the Mayo girls had. This would be a contest, that was certain.

The siren went and the ball was thrown up. For 47 seconds, Cora savoured where she was and the journey that had brought her there. She remembered her mother's vow to witness her playing in Croke Park, after their first visit to the Mater Hospital. In the end, her mam never got the chance. But her dad was in the stands today, watching Cora's first All-Ireland final with the Mayo seniors, and that was something.

Far too soon, she saw a substitute, Orla, running onto the pitch. Orla gave the referee a slip of paper and sprinted up to Cora's corner. It was time for Cora to make way. Using her good arm, she gave Orla a high-five as she jogged to the sideline.

Usually when Cora played a match, it flew by, but being on the sideline was completely different. The minutes crawled past. It was a tight, tense match. There was only ever a point or two between the teams. Cora kept hoping for a Mayo goal, for something to break the game open, but the Waterford keeper was good.

Cora felt utterly helpless on the bench. She couldn't sit still in the dugout. She had to pace up and down the sideline to burn off some bit of energy. She roared herself hoarse, even though she knew that because of the crowd, the girls wouldn't be able to hear her.

Gradually, in the second half, Mayo began to pull away. They were able to stay going a bit longer than Waterford. All those tough training sessions, the endless Up and Downs, started to pay off. Cora could see how tired the girls were and yet they kept going. The gap widened to two points, to three. Then, in the dying minutes, Sinéad kicked over a beauty to seal it.

The siren at full-time was one of the sweetest sounds Cora had ever heard. Along with the management team and subs, she invaded the pitch, screaming and hugging every player she met. She had never known such pure glee.

She watched Diane lift the Brendan Martin Cup and make a heartfelt speech.

She watched Marcella take a fistful of grass from the sod: 'I don't want to leave!' she kept saying. The homecoming to Mayo would be something else.

'This won't be our last All-Ireland,' she said to Crazy as they walked around the perimeter of the pitch, soaking it up.

'Definitely not,' said Crazy.

Next time, Cora vowed to herself, she would be on the pitch when they won.

CHAPTER 16

BACK TO BACK

Cora somehow managed to fit studying for her Leaving Cert around all her football commitments. Studying wasn't really her thing – anytime she tried to sit still and concentrate, her thoughts drifted to football – but she had her heart set on a course in Sport & Recreation in Athlone IT, so she put in the work.

A course like that would allow her to get involved in sport during her working life as well, so even when she retired from playing, sport could still be central to her life. Crazy was applying for the same course, and if they both got in they would live in the same house. Cora felt much better about leaving home and heading off to college knowing that she had a friend with her. One thing was certain – life with Crazy would never be boring!

They both got the points they needed and celebrated like mad for a few days before settling back into their normal training schedule. All the Mayo girls were determined to make it back to Croke Park in September to win the double. That meant not just training hard but looking after themselves, too – eating healthy food, getting a good night's sleep, going to the pool after matches to help their muscles recover.

When Cora and Crazy arrived in Athlone, they both received sports scholarships, which was a huge financial boost. Cora felt proud that she was able to contribute to her rent and fees, and take some of the pressure off her dad. Herself and Crazy both started playing for the college team. Cora felt less pressure playing for Athlone than she did for Carnacon and Mayo; she was able to enjoy it purely for the football.

She missed home sometimes, but she was also thrilled to be striking out on her own. And if she ever got lonely, Crazy wasn't long in cheering her up.

★

Two weeks after starting college, Mayo were back in the All-Ireland final. Once again, they faced Waterford. Despite the fact that they had won the year before, all the media reports were backing Waterford to win. Finbar used this as motivation in the training sessions leading up to the final.

'Last year counts for nothing in their eyes!' he yelled, brandishing one of the Sunday broadsheets. 'They don't believe in ye, girls. They don't respect ye. Well, this is what I think of them.' He ripped the paper up in front of them, and they all cheered.

On the bus to Croke Park, Cora could sense that the mood was a lot calmer this year. On All-Ireland final day, the occasion could get to you – the stadium, the crowd, the fancy dressing rooms. Even the little rituals like meeting the President or walking behind the Artane Band could distract you from your game. But they'd been through it all before and knew what to expect.

Despite all this, Cora could feel every nerve in her body sparking. She told herself she wasn't nervous; she was just ready for action. When she pulled on her brand-new jersey in the dressing room, she knew it was now or never.

She was happy with her first-half performance – she nabbed a goal and a point. She felt a sense of relief when the goal hit the net. *I'm settled now,* she thought. But she also knew she couldn't rest on her laurels. There were more goals to be scored.

Waterford were up by a point at half-time, but just like the previous year, there was a sense of calm in the dressing room.

'Let's just keep doing what we're doing, girls,' Cora said. 'We know we'll be able to finish strong, we'll have the legs. We didn't run all those Up and Downs for nothing!'

Halfway through the second half, Maria won the ball on the 20-metre line and turned her player. She seemed to be straight through on goal when the corner-back came out of nowhere and hauled her down. The ref blew his whistle and held his arms out straight: penalty.

Immediately, Crazy ran over to Cora. They had been practising penalties together in Athlone for weeks: Cora would take a shot on Crazy, then they'd swap and Crazy would take a shot on Cora.

During these practice sessions, Crazy had scored more goals. Cora maintained that this was because Crazy was the better goalkeeper, not the better penalty-taker! But nonetheless, Crazy's confidence was flying high, and Cora knew she'd be well able to handle the pressure.

'You've got this,' Cora said, handing Crazy the ball.

Crazy placed it on the spot and took five steps back. She used the same technique every time, but Cora was never able to tell which way she'd kick it. She approached the ball and calmly slotted it past the Waterford keeper. Cora let out a yell of delight. It turned out that watching your best friend score a goal in an All-Ireland final was almost as good as scoring yourself.

Waterford weren't done, though. They'd been All-Ireland champions themselves and they knew how to win. Nothing rattled them, not even goals – they just kept tagging on point after point. As the clock counted down, Waterford managed to put themselves in front by three points.

Cora knew something special was needed to wrestle this game back for Mayo. She'd been through so much and worked so hard – she wasn't going to give up now.

The ball came bouncing down the wing and Cora latched onto it. She took on her marker, swivelled, and kicked it over the bar. The Mayo crowd roared its approval.

They were in the dying moments now. Another low ball came down the wing, almost a carbon copy of the previous one. Cora won it again. She turned to kick another point but noticed the Waterford keeper was off her line. Cora judged her kick; she wanted it to dip in at crossbar height.

The ball snuck in under the crossbar and the crowd went wild.

Cora knew there was no time to celebrate. 'Let's defend now, girls!' she shouted, running out to midfield.

The goal had put Mayo a point in front. Waterford pressed again and won a free. It looked like it might be the last kick of the game. It wasn't a difficult free, but it wasn't an easy one either – about forty yards out, just to the left of the goals.

As the Waterford freetaker approached the ball, Cora held her breath. The ball shaved the post. The umpire waved his arms emphatically – it was wide!

When the siren sounded, Cora and Crazy ran to each other and jumped around the place, hugging and screaming. They had done it! Cora had won her second All-Ireland medal, but this time she'd been right in the thick of it. Cora's blood, sweat and tears had gone into winning this match, and the victory was all the sweeter for it.

Just like the previous year, she lingered on the pitch as long as she could. There was no feeling that could compare to this. She was surrounded by teammates, friends, family and supporters. The last ten months of hard work had all been worth it.

'We did it!' she and her teammates kept saying to each other, in amazement.

It felt incredible to be able to take the cup back over the Shannon to Mayo for a second year running. In the days after the final, they toured all over the county – from Ballyhaunis to Belmullet, Westport to Claremorris. It was a week before Cora came up for air. She never wanted this feeling to end.

★

After the madness of the All-Ireland celebrations had died down, she and Crazy were on a bus to Dublin, headed to Trinity College for a blitz with Athlone. Cora was looking forward to it. Now that the pressure of the All-Ireland was off, she could just run out on the pitch, express herself and have fun.

In their second game of the day against Maynooth, she was battling for the ball in a ruck when she collided with another player. Cora saw stars. She sank to the ground. There was a throbbing pain in her jaw like the worst toothache imaginable. The world began to seem very far away. Cora sank into blackness.

Next thing she knew, she was in the Mater Hospital and the pain had subsided a bit. Crazy was sitting by her bed.

'I made sure they gave you some good painkillers,' she said with a grin.

Crazy told her what had happened. When Cora had been fighting for the ball, she'd lowered her head. The side of her face had collided with the shoulder of a Maynooth player and her jaw had shattered.

'You dropped like a sack of spuds,' Crazy informed her. 'You blacked out with the pain.'

'That makes sense,' mumbled Cora. 'I don't remember much.'

'You were stretchered off and everything. It was very dramatic. The poor Maynooth girl was in bits.'

'Ah, it was a pure accident,' said Cora.

There was no chance of Cora returning to Athlone as planned. She stayed the night at her sister Collette's and the next day, a Friday, she checked into the Dublin Dental University Hospital. A surgery to rebuild her jaw was scheduled for that evening. She met the surgeon in the afternoon.

'Will I be able to leave tomorrow? Or Sunday?' she asked with difficulty.

The surgeon frowned. 'Probably not. Ideally, we'd keep you for a few nights …'

'I'd like to leave on Sunday if at all possible.'

'What's your hurry?'

'The All-Stars are on,' she admitted. The banquet was fixed for that Sunday, and it was the first time Cora had been nominated. She had a dress bought and everything.

The surgeon grinned. 'We'll see what we can do.'

The morning after Cora's surgery, Crazy came in to visit. 'How are you feeling?' she asked.

'Sore,' Cora admitted. She was trying to eat a bowl of jelly that the nurses had brought her, but her whole face was aching.

Crazy held up a shopping bag. 'A present from my mam. Enough liquidised meals to last you a week.'

'Your mam is a legend,' said Cora.

Crazy sat down. 'The glamorous life of a county footballer, eh?'

Cora laughed, then quickly stopped – even laughing hurt. 'I'm just glad it happened after the All-Ireland. Can you imagine if I'd missed another final?'

In the end, the hospital released Cora in time for the All-Stars. Her sisters Sheena and Collette did her hair and makeup and Crazy drove her to the ceremony. At the banquet, Cora looked longingly at everyone else tucking into their beef dinners, but on the other hand she was just happy to be there at all.

Then the formalities got underway and players started being called to the stage. It was mostly Mayo and Waterford players, but some Tyrone players received awards too. They got to the inside forwardline and Cora heard her name being called. Nerves flared in her chest; even though she was used to being the centre of attention on the pitch, she was always uneasy at public occasions like this. She got up carefully from her table and walked to the stage – she was still a bit woozy from her pain medication.

She received her award and turned to look at the crowd. They had all risen in a standing ovation. It was incredible to see her fellow players honour her in this way. Cora thought her heart would burst.

CHAPTER 17

AISLING

The next few years were a flurry of activity for Cora, playing for Carnacon and Mayo and studying in Athlone. Before she knew it, she was celebrating the milestone of her 21st birthday. She had a big party in the local in Carnacon. A covers band from Castlebar played all her favourite songs and her sisters baked a huge round cake and iced it to look like a football. They stayed out till the small hours. All her teammates were there to celebrate with her and it reminded her of nights out after victories – everyone happy, everyone together.

There had been ups and downs the last few years, but Cora now had three senior All-Ireland medals to her name. Last year, 2001, had been a blip in her career. They had reached the All-Ireland final for the third year in a row, and they were all geared up to do the treble. The final against Laois had been a tight, high-scoring match. Laois opened up a lead in the second half but Mayo pulled it slowly back. With a minute left, Cora equalised with a long-range free. She felt like a hero – but about thirty seconds later she was the villain. She gave away a silly free within range of the Mayo goal and the Laois freetaker made no mistake. Mayo lost by that single point, and Cora still sometimes had nightmares about that day.

So this year she had been determined to redeem herself. She kicked eight points in the All-Ireland final against Monaghan, another tight game that they won by a single point. It was Mayo's third All-Ireland in four years, but to Cora it may as well have been their first, such was the joy and relief she felt.

The real icing on the cake was that Carnacon reached the All-Ireland club final too. Cora was captain and felt so intensely proud of her clubmates, especially the young ones coming through: fifteen-year-old Fiona McHale was a dangerous corner-forward, and Aisling McGing, Michelle's younger sister, was flying it at wing-back. They met Carrickmore of Tyrone in the final. Carnacon played into the wind in the first half and had built up a good lead at half-time, including 1-5 from Cora herself. Carrickmore fought back, coming within two points, but when a short kickout by their keeper was intercepted, Fiona latched onto it and kicked it into the net.

Winning All-Irelands with Mayo felt amazing, but reaching the pinnacle with her club – the girls she'd grown up with and trained alongside for years – was something else. When the final whistle went, it seemed that the entire village of Carnacon invaded the pitch. Cora caught sight of Jimmy in the crowd: tears of happiness were streaming down his face. Cora had wanted to win for Jimmy and Beatrice as much as herself. They'd done so much for her over the years, bringing her to games, constantly supporting and believing in her, and being there for her when her mam died. They'd almost been like a second set of parents.

At the homecoming in Carnacon, Cora felt like everything had come full circle. Her primary school principal Mr Ó Súilleabháin was the MC. Her old friend Alan Dillon from her days with the Ballintubber boys team was also there in support. He was on the Mayo senior football panel now, and they swapped war stories late into the night.

So when Cora had her 21st in December 2002, it wasn't just her birthday she was celebrating. When it came to football, she was, quite simply, on top of the world.

In the summer of 2003, they met Laois in the national league. Cora had never quite forgiven Laois for the 2001 All-Ireland final and so she was always determined to beat them whenever they met. Just before half-time she was running at the Laois backs, hunting for a goal. She planted her foot and tried to go past her marker; her foot went one way, her knee the other. She could have sworn she heard a popping noise just before she crumpled to the ground. Her knee swelled up instantly, like a cartoon, and the pain was off the charts.

Even though she'd already been through the

wringer with her collarbone and her jaw, Cora knew her injury troubles were far from over. She had torn her cruciate ligament, an important tissue that connects the muscles above and below the knee. The doctors told her she'd need surgery but that would put her out for the year, and Cora wasn't willing to miss out on another All-Ireland. Crazy had had surgery on her cruciate the year before and was only coming back from it now.

The only other option was to work through the pain and try and build up her knee as best she could. She did physio exercises every day to make her knee as strong as it could be. She wore a bulky knee brace that supported the torn ligament but also slowed her down. Plus, it looked a bit ridiculous. Crazy took to calling her the Bionic Woman.

Because they were both recovering from injury, Finbar asked Cora and Crazy to manage the Mayo Minors. Neither of them was able to play for a while, so this would be a good distraction. Cora got a huge kick out of it. The players were all so enthusiastic and energetic – they reminded her of herself when she was younger. Fiona and Aisling from Carnacon were both on the Minor team. Aisling in particular was the star of the team and definitely the biggest messer on the squad. Herself and Crazy had a natural rapport. Aisling told them that she was hoping to go to Athlone to study hairdressing when she finished her Leaving Cert that summer.

'Why don't you move into our house?' Crazy suggested.

'Ah, ye'd only lead me astray!' Aisling shot back, laughing.

Cora enjoyed management, but she also found it frustrating. You could prepare a team as best you could and give a brilliant dressing-room speech, but once the whistle was blown, you could do very little. The experience reminded her of her first All-Ireland with Mayo, when she was injured and had prowled the sidelines, urging the girls on but feeling utterly helpless. Still, they were a good bunch, and with Aisling leading the charge, Cora felt confident that the Minors could win an All-Ireland of their own.

Then, out of the blue, tragedy struck.

Cora was coming off the field after beating Galway

on a glorious July day when a Mayo supporter approached her and asked her to go find Michelle and her sister Sharon. Aisling had been in a car accident, the man said, and was in hospital. Cora went into the dressing room and told the girls, her voice shaking. Herself and Crazy went with Michelle and Sharon to the hospital in Castlebar.

When they arrived, they pieced the story together: Aisling had gotten a lift to the Galway match to support her sisters. Along the way, the car she was travelling in had collided with another. The drivers of both cars were okay, but Aisling's injuries were critical. She had woken up briefly and spoken to her parents, but beyond that it was touch and go.

Cora and Crazy stayed in the waiting area near Aisling's room as friends, teammates and family members filtered in and out. They fetched teas and coffees and went out for food to keep everyone's energy up. As the evening went on, Cora's hope grew. Aisling would pull through, she thought. Of course she would. She was tough as nails, full of life, and had everything to live for. Why wouldn't she pull through?

Later that night, Cora was dozing in her chair

when she heard the sound of crying. She opened her eyes and knew without being told that Aisling had died.

Aisling's was the biggest funeral that Cora had ever attended. Along with other Carnacon and Mayo players, she formed a guard of honour for the funeral procession. Aisling's number 5 Carnacon jersey was draped over her coffin. When Cora saw that, a lump rose in her throat.

In the days and weeks that followed, she tried to be there for Aisling's sisters as much as possible. Michelle, in particular, was one of her oldest friends; they'd been through so much together. Sometimes Michelle felt numb, sometimes angry, sometimes deeply sad. Cora had gone through similar emotions when her mam died. This time, there was shock on top of everything else. It was so sudden and it made no sense. Aisling was talented and funny and had everything going for her. All her potential, gone in the space of day. None of it made any sense.

In the wake of Aisling's death, Cora had dozens

of conversations with her friends and teammates who had known Aisling. They remembered her and told funny stories. They talked openly to each other about their hopes and fears and aspirations. About how life was short. In some ways, Cora knew, they had never been closer as a team.

When they got to the All-Ireland final against Dublin two months later, both Michelle and Sharon were starting, having played brilliantly in the run-up to the final. Cora was so proud of them, in awe of their strength and composure.

With two minutes to go, it didn't look good – Dublin were leading by two points. Cora's injury was bothering her and she'd had a quiet game. When she got a free on the 45, she knew what to do: she lobbed it in. The ball broke to Diane, who kicked it into the roof of the net. When the siren went, Cora burst into tears. She'd won her fourth All-Ireland medal, and this was the most meaningful of them all.

The whole team gathered around Michelle and Sharon and hugged them fiercely. They'd done it again, and this time they'd done it for Aisling.

CHAPTER 18

A CHANGE OF CAREER

Cora didn't know it at the time, but Mayo's success in 2003 would be their last for a long while. The following year was Finbar's last season in charge. They wanted to win another All-Ireland to give him a good send-off, but they lost in the semi-final to a determined Galway team who went on to claim the cup. The year after that, they were beaten in the semi-final by a young Cork side who pipped them by a point in the last minute.

It was Cork's first time getting to an All-Ireland final, but it wouldn't be their last.

Mayo couldn't really settle with a manager after Finbar, and they never found the magical combination of luck, personnel and confidence needed to win another All-Ireland. Slowly, the winning atmosphere seeped out of the camp. Cora kept training and kept trying, as did her teammates. Her managers were well-meaning and dedicated, but sometimes Cora felt that they didn't listen to the players. She also felt that the county board made decisions that were occasionally hard to fathom. Managers came and went, but the players remained, and they were the ones who had to live with the board's decisions. She still loved the game, but it felt like they weren't making any progress.

And Cork were so good, and so dominant. The young, determined team that had knocked out Mayo in 2005 would go on to win eleven All-Ireland titles in twelve years. That happened in sport, sometimes – a power emerged, a county that became the team to beat. It had been Mayo for five years, and now it was Cork.

Mayo did make it to the 2007 final against Cork, who were then gunning for three in a row. Only seven Mayo players remained from their first title in 1999, including Cora, Christina, Marcella, Crazy and Claire. Cora was thrilled for younger players like Fiona who were getting their first outing in Croke Park. But the game itself was incredibly frustrating. Cora was marked by two or three girls at all times and found it hard to get on the ball. She managed to sneak a late goal, but Mayo still lost by five points. More frustrating still was the feeling that they hadn't prepared properly. They would have made a better fist of it, Cora reckoned, if Finbar had still been around.

Strangely enough, Cora liked many of the Cork players – they were down to earth, and always friendly when they met socially. They were committed and supportive of each other in a way that reminded Cora of different Mayo and Carnacon teams she'd been a part of.

'It'd be easier if they weren't so sound,' Crazy remarked one night on an All-Star tour, after they'd hung out with the Cork girls.

Cora laughed. 'I know what you mean.'

If Mayo was in decline, Carnacon was on the rise. In the space of eight years, the club reached seven All-Ireland finals, winning four. Success was addictive, and Cora chased it with all her might. Winning with her club made the long seasons and the tough training sessions all worth it.

Off the pitch, Cora found great satisfaction in her work. Because of sport, she'd always had an interest in health and wellbeing. Being a great footballer wasn't just about training; she also made sure to eat healthy foods, drinks lots of water and get plenty of sleep each night. So in 2007 she went back to college in Galway to study Health Promotion, which would allow her to work in the community, educating people about health issues and helping them to change their lifestyles for the better.

After she graduated, she got a job promoting health and wellbeing among Mayo's Travelling community. She loved working with Traveller women in particular; they were interested in the skills Cora taught them, and she knew they would pass this knowledge on to other members of their community. They were chatty and warm, too, and Cora enjoyed listening to their stories. Sometimes she was shocked at the abuse that some of her clients received on the street, just for being Travellers. Cora got dirty looks, too, just for being seen with them! But she loved her job, so she was able to shrug off the ignorant comments. She knew that her work made a difference, and that gave her great satisfaction.

Cora also finally did the sensible thing and had her cruciate ligament operated on. Her knee kept locking up in the middle of matches and she knew she couldn't put it off any longer. The operation meant that she had to miss the All-Star tour to Dubai — but she didn't miss any matches, and that was the most important thing.

Then, in 2017, something changed.

First of all, Mayo got a new manager. Frank was the same age as Cora's father and had the same gentle demeanour. He was from Wexford and more of a hurling man than anything else.

'He'll never work out,' Cora said to Crazy after their first meeting with Frank.

'I don't know. He seems genuine.'

'Yeah, but hurling?' Cora made a face. Hurling may have been popular in other parts of the country, but in Mayo it was football all the way.

But Frank surprised her. He was very different to Finbar, who was brash and confident; Frank was thoughtful about sport and very tactically aware. They reached the semi-final against Cork, who were hunting their seventh title in a row. The whole panel was energised by the thought of stopping Cork. They prepared mentally and physically with an intensity that Cora hadn't seen in years. Cora herself spent long hours in the gym and on the physio's table, slowly building back up her knee after her operation. As a panel, they knew they would have to work harder than ever before to beat this exceptional Cork team.

At half-time, it seemed like their plan was working. They led by two points but they had also squandered a few goal chances. Cora had managed to power home a goal off her left foot just before the break, but she'd kicked her fair share of wides too.

'You can't miss chances against a team like Cork,' Cora told them in the dressing room. 'They have a winning mentality, they'll exploit every weakness, they'll never stop believing they can win it. We have to be mentally tougher than them now and we *have* to take our chances up front. Are we ready to do that?'

The girls shouted back that they were. Then they went out and proved it. They scored two goals in the second half to put themselves ahead by two points with five minutes to go. But as Cora knew from experience, two points was the most danger-ous lead.

Then, disaster struck and a Cork player was pulled down in the square. Crazy was in the goals that day, and as she stared down the penalty-taker, Cora prayed.

It was a good penalty, low and tucked into the corner, but Crazy managed to get down and get a hand to it. Cora punched the air – Mayo were still in it! In the dying minutes, the ball came down Cora's way and she managed to kick over a secu-rity point. When the siren went, they screamed and jumped and celebrated. They were in another All-Ireland final!

Later that evening, Cora, Crazy and Martha went to the pub together. It had been ten years since they'd last been in Croke Park together; fourteen years since they'd won the title. They were all in their thirties now, and sometimes their younger teammates liked to slag them about when they were going to retire.

'What do you think?' Martha asked. 'Do we still have it in us?'

'Of course we have!' said Cora.

As Crazy was leaving them for the night, she turned back with a smile on her face. 'One more shot at glory, so?'

'One more shot,' said Cora.

The buildup to the final reminded Cora of their very first All-Ireland in 1999. The people of Mayo were hungry for success and were backing both the men's and women's teams to bring the cup home from Croker in September.

The Mayo ladies panel travelled as a group to watch the men play in their final against Dublin. Cora soaked up the atmosphere and tried to relax. In a week's time, it would be her out on the pitch, also facing Dublin. It was an exciting time in Mayo football, and Cora hoped that they would make the most of it.

Her old teammate Alan was part of the Mayo squad that day. It was an incredibly close game, and neither team led by much more than a point at any stage. Dublin were seeking their third in a row, whereas Mayo were going for their first men's All-Ireland win since 1951. Somewhere, in the back of Cora's mind, were thoughts of the Mayo curse.

In the 76th minute, the sides were level. Dublin got a free around the 45-metre line. Dean Rock stood over it. As a fellow freetaker, Cora studied his body language with interest. She could tell he was confident and focused. He slotted it over, and Dublin were All-Ireland champions for the third year running.

In the stands, Cora put her face in her hands. It was agonising to see the lads fall short again when they clearly had the talent and drive to win. *Is it ever going to go our way?* she wondered.

As they shuffled out of the grounds, dejected, Crazy turned to her with a look of determination. 'Just in case we needed any more motivation,' she said.

★

She knew Dublin would be no pushover. They had played in the last three finals in a row, losing to Cork on each occasion. They were young and energetic and they'd had enough of heartbreak. But Cora knew that Mayo, too, would be hungry.

They were playing in front of the biggest crowd to ever attend a ladies football final – almost fifty thousand people. Waiting in the tunnel, Cora could feel the noise of the crowd vibrating in her bones. For the warmup she was totally focused, but when they walked behind the band she took the opportunity to take everything in. She looked at the perfect grass and couldn't help but smile. She had missed playing here.

Even though she was playing at full-forward, Cora went in for the throw-up. She loved being there at the start, right in the cauldron. Within five minutes she had fisted over her first point and felt herself settle. She then landed a long-range free from outside the 45 and felt her confidence grow. She couldn't believe the roar from the crowd.

The teams were neck and neck, but after twenty

minutes, Dublin slotted home a goal. Shortly afterwards Crazy was sin-binned for pulling down a Dublin forward in the square. Luckily the sub-goalie, Aisling, made a brilliant save on the penalty, but Mayo were still in trouble. Cora had scored three points in the first half, but she'd also kicked a few wides and she cursed those wasted chances.

They were a goal down at half-time. In the dressing room, they promised each other they'd leave it all on the pitch. It didn't need to be said that this might be the last appearance in a Mayo jersey for some of them. They all understood, and they all vowed to give everything for each other.

They started the second half solidly, but it seemed that every point Mayo pulled back, Dublin answered. Cora got a massive point halfway through the second half only for Dublin to respond almost straightaway. With eight minutes to go, there was still only a goal between them. Then Dublin seemed to flick a switch. They got three goals in quick succession and pulled away. Cora got a few late frees and dropped them in to try and engineer a goal, but nothing came. She knew before the siren that the game was gone.

Cora didn't think it would hurt as much as her first All-Ireland loss, but if anything it hurt more. Now that she was nearing the end of her career, everything meant more. She sat on the grass and watched the Dublin girls lift the cup. Her nieces ran onto the pitch to comfort her, and they at least could make her smile. She hoped that some day she'd be in the stands watching them on the field of play.

In the dressing room, she and Crazy and Martha sat together. They had all been down the same road together, and they understood each other. Cora felt terrible for the girls on the team who had just lost their first All-Ireland – they were crying the hardest. As for Cora, she just felt so tired.

After a while, she spoke to the group. She told them all to stick together and come back stronger. When she was growing up, she told them, she had only a few female footballers to look up to. Now she thought of her nieces and the fact that they had loads of heroines to inspire them. That made Cora proud.

★

Soon after the All-Ireland defeat, Cora began to think seriously about a change in her sporting career. For a few months, she'd been in touch with a Cavan man named Nick Walsh who was a scout for the WAFL – the newly formed women's Aussie Rules league. He told her that the Greater Western Giants, who were based in Sydney, were interested in signing her.

Cora was torn. On the one hand, she loved the idea of heading over to a sunny climate to play sport professionally, but on the other, how could she leave her teammates and family behind? Besides, what did she really know about Aussie Rules? Based on what she'd seen on telly, you could take six steps with the ball in your hand instead of four; there were no goalkeepers; there were four quarters in the game instead of two halves; and they played with a rugby ball.

Nick gave her one of the balls to try out. Sherrin was the brand; the Australian version of O'Neills, she supposed. She took it down to the pitch in Carnacon to try it out. Straightaway, she could see it was going to take her a while to get used to it. With the oddly shaped ball, the bounce was wild and unpredictable. And she was going to have to adjust her way of kicking, too. With a round football, she could do all kinds of tricks: curl it, spin it, angle it with great precision. But the Sherrin ball didn't behave in the same way. She was a good Gaelic footballer all right, but there was no guarantee she'd be a good Australian footballer!

She began texting and emailing with the Giants' coach, an energetic grey-haired man named Alan McConnell, who was a former Aussie Rules player himself. He made it clear to her that he didn't just want her for her football ability, but for her experience and winning mentality.

Eventually, he convinced her to fly out to Sydney for a trial. On the plane, she was full of nervous excitement. *Life is funny*, she thought to herself. *One minute you think your career is nearing its end; the next, a mad opportunity like this one shows up!*

Alan met her at the airport. She was jetlagged and exhausted but still happy to meet him. He talked non-stop about his plans for the Giants' season and why he was so keen to make her the first international signing in the WAFL.

He took her straight to the Giants' facilities to

give her a tour. Cora was still adjusting to the heat and brightness of the Australian climate – not to mention the accents! – but she could see that it was a top-class facility. There was an impressive gym, comfortable dressing rooms that were even fancier than the ones in Croke Park, several AstroTurf pitches and a huge pool. Even better, the men's and women's teams shared everything, and Cora could see male and female players joking around with each other as they worked out with punchbags and kettlebells. It was a far cry from the GAA, where the women's code played second fiddle to the men's. It had annoyed Cora, at times, seeing what the Mayo men got in comparison to the women: more gear, more prominent pitches and fixtures, and better facilities. But here, everything was shared equally.

Despite her exhaustion, Alan insisted that she run through a skills session with him while another coach filmed the whole thing. For ninety minutes, Cora kicked, caught and chased the strangely shaped ball. Even though she knew they were interested in her, Cora still felt a strong desire to prove herself. After a while, she was aware that she had an audience – a few of the male players, plus their coach

Leon Cameron, had wandered over for a look. Cora wondered what they made of her, a Gaelic footballer from Ireland, over here trying to play their sport.

After a moment, Leon called over to Alan: 'You'd be mad not to sign her, mate!'

A few days later, Cora was back in Ireland. She'd signed a contract and her future with the Giants in Sydney was secured. The next few weeks, however, would be all about Carnacon as they tried to capture a sixth club All-Ireland title. It felt fitting that she do this before heading off to a new life in Australia; her clubmates had been the ones who had kept her going all these years.

One more shot at glory, as Crazy would say. One more shot.

SYDNEY

Cora could never get used to the long-haul flights to Australia. No matter how many movies she watched or how many naps she took, she still found them tough going. But this plane journey was a breeze. Carnacon had won their sixth All-Ireland club title, and she was reliving every moment in her head. It was better than any sort of in-flight entertainment.

Now she was heading to Sydney for four months to play in her first season of WAFL. She would spend Christmas with her brother Brian, who lived in Sydney, her sister-in-law Denise, and her little nephews Cian and Jack. She couldn't wait to see them all again.

She was excited to start playing Aussie Rules properly, but this didn't mean she was done with the round ball. She'd return to Ireland in the spring to play ladies football again. She didn't know how long she could keep juggling both codes, but she was willing to try.

Cora quickly settled in to life in Sydney as a pro athlete. She loved being able to train every day; to practise her kicking in 'The Cage', the Giants' specially designed kicking facility; and to focus entirely on sport. She was also getting paid, which meant a lot to her. Growing up, she'd idolised professional sportspeople like Sonia O'Sullivan, Ronan O'Gara and Roy Keane. She envied them, the way they were able to commit to their sport full-time. Now it was happening to her. She loved her job as a health promoter back home, but being able to focus her mind and her body on sport all day was an incredible privilege.

Cora was often shy around new people, but the Giants girls had made her feel really welcome.

They were amazed at her movement and vision, her ability to spot a gap in the defence. Coming from Gaelic, she had a different approach, and they were as eager to learn from her as she was from them. She was still adjusting to the new ball, the rock-hard pitches, and the rugby-like tackles. She couldn't get over the professional setup: the video analysis, statistics, dietary advice, motivational talks, even apps on their phones dedicated to training.

She had her own apartment in the city near Brian and his family, and a car to get to and from training. She loved being able to reconnect with Brian and get to know her nephews. They spent Christmas day hanging out on the beach, having a barbeque instead of turkey and ham. It was bliss.

Finally, the day of her first WAFL match arrived. She was a little bit nervous and incredibly excited – or else the other way around, she couldn't decide! The previous week, Alan had handed her the jersey that would be hers for the duration of her Giants career. She laughed. It was number 13.

'Now, some say it's unlucky …' Alan began.

Cora cut him off. 'Don't worry. I'm well used to wearing this number!'

Now she was in the dressing room with the other girls, getting ready for the game against Melbourne. It felt strange to be pulling on an orange singlet instead of the green and red jersey of Mayo and Carnacon. But the singlet reminded her that what she was doing was new and exciting. A new challenge.

It was a different sport, and she was a different player here. Her footwork was faster than the other girls were used to. They were amazed at her ball-winning ability. They threw stats at her and half the time she didn't know what they were on about. They even slagged her about her accent!

But it was sport, and sport was what she loved. At the end of the day, it was about pulling on a jersey and giving it her best. She'd done that for Ballin-tubber, for Carnacon, for Mayo, and now for the Giants in Sydney. As she ran out on the pitch to the roars of the crowd, she couldn't help but smile in the searing Australian sun. This was what she was born to do.

CORA STAUNTON'S ACHIEVEMENTS

Age at debut for Mayo senior ladies football: 13

Age at debut for Greater Western Sydney Giants: 36

Six-time club All-Ireland winner with Carnacon
(2002, 2007, 2008, 2011, 2013, 2017)

Three-time National League winner with Mayo
(2000, 2004, 2007)

Four-time All-Ireland winner with Mayo (1999,
2000, 2002, 2003)

Eleven-time All-Star (2000, 2001, 2002, 2004, 2007,
2008, 2009, 2012, 2013, 2015, 2017)

Appearances for Greater Western Sydney Giants: 14
(2018–19)

ALSO AVAILABLE

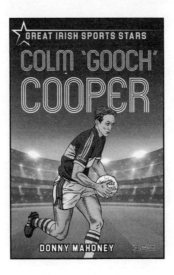

The Gaelic footballer who's won nearly every prize in the game:
Including 5 All-Irelands & 8 All-Stars

How a boy who everyone said wasn't big enough or strong
enough to wear the green and gold jersey of Kerry became one of
the greatest Gaelic footballers of all time.